HOT DAMN!

ALSO
BY JAMES W. HALL

THRILLERS

Blackwater Sound
Rough Draft
Body Language
Red Sky at Night
Buzz Cut
Gone Wild
Mean High Tide
Hard Aground
Bones of Coral
Tropical Freeze
Under Cover of Daylight

POETRY

The Lady from the Dark Green Hills
Ham Operator
False Statements
The Mating Reflex

SHORT STORIES

Paper Products

JAMES W. HALL

ST. MARTIN'S PRESS   NEW YORK

HOT DAMN!

ALLIGATORS IN THE CASINO

NUDE WOMEN IN THE GRASS

HOW SEASHELLS CHANGED
THE COURSE OF HISTORY

and Other Dispatches from Paradise

www.stmartins.com

Illustrations © William Rosado 2001

Design by Susan Walsh

Library of Congress Cataloging-in-Publication Data

Hall, James W. (James Wilson)
    Hot Damn! Alligators in the casino, Nude women in the grass, How seashells changed the course of history, and other dispatches from paradise / James W. Hall.—1st. ed.
    p.cm.
    ISBN 0-312-28859-X
    1. Hall, James W. (James Wilson)—Homes and haunts—Florida. 2. Authors, American—20th century—Biography 3. Florida—Social life and customs. I. Title.

PS3558 A369 Z467 2002
814'54—dc21

                                        200158563

First Edition: June 2002

10 9 8 7 6 5 4 3 2 1

With love to my mother,
Anne Hall

CONTENTS

CONTENTS

ACKNOWLEDGMENTS

The author wishes to thank the *Washington Post*, the *Miami Herald*, and the *Ft. Lauderdale Sun-Sentinel*, where these works first appeared.

INTRODUCTION

Essays are about as sexy as donkeys. They slog along in the muck and mire, saddled with the tedious burdens that the finer animals in the stable would never be asked to carry. Who would write an essay to win the heart of another, or use the form to cry out in the hour of deepest grief? Poems are for that, lean-muscled thoroughbreds racing with their minuscule load to some lyrical finish line. At least this was my belief for most of my adult life.

I suppose college composition classes are partly to blame for turning us against the essay form. Compare and contrast, analysis, argument. Four years of that and most sane humans would avoid essays for the rest of their natural lives. Who in their right mind would ever voluntarily sit down and write one of the things?

Not so with the other literary forms.

It is not unusual for a poet to write hundreds upon hundreds of poems that are never seen beyond the poet's family yet still keep writing. Successful novelists frequently write four or five failed novels before their first one is published, and there are some writers who are this day slaving away on their twentieth novel still without even a faintly positive rejection letter. No one is paying them to do it, no one is chumming the waters of their ego. They simply feel compelled. They feel a need, a drive, a desperate joy, and they forge on despite the rejection, despite the great odds against them. They write because the writing of a novel is the utmost challenge they know, an Everest that by golly they are determined to get to the top of, if for no other reason than simply to see the view from a structure four hundred pages high.

Do essay writers feel such rapture? Are they driven by an equal need? Or is it such a left brain activity, such a chore to create a logical and rigorously coherent construct, that no such bliss is biologically possible? For most of my life I religiously avoided the form. So when a young newspaper editor by the name of Dave Wieczorek called one day and offered me a job writing a monthly personal essay for their Sunday magazine, my first reaction was a derisive snort. He said I could write about anything I wanted. It should have a Florida orientation, but otherwise I was free to roam. And even the Florida thing wasn't chiseled in marble. Would I at least think about it? There was a nice chunk of change involved.

Oh, all right then. Still deeply skeptical, I told him I'd try one or two, see how it went. No promises, no long-term commitment. Having spent thirty-odd years tending the gardens of poetry and fiction writing, I was totally unpracticed in the form, not to mention biased against it. I struggled mightily through the first one, which starts off this collection. I wasn't sure what the newspaper folks wanted, but more important, I wasn't sure what the form was capable of delivering. I put aside all my other projects and focused on that damn stubborn mulish creature that I had to tug and cajole and prod up the mountain of four pages.

Somewhere along that steep trail my donkey and I found a rhythm. We caught our strides and what had seemed nigh onto impossible in the first paragraph was suddenly an effortless pleasure. A sweet wind was in our face. We were galloping, by god, almost airborne. And thus began a three-year love affair with the essay form.

Not since the heyday of my poetry career had I had such regular jolts of satisfaction and pleasure while writing. Novels take me at least a year to complete, and a lot of that time is spent hauling stone blocks up the face of a pyramid, then chipping away the ragged excess so each stone fits into place. It's work and work and work, a lot of heavy lifting. Oh, sure, a novel has its moments of utter delight. Complex problems solved, characters saying and doing marvelously unforeseen things, the small bombshells of discovery. Ah-ha, so this is what the story is all about! But with a thousand-word essay packaged in four tightly woven pages, the pleasure comes in the same way it does with the completion of a successful poem. Yeats described it as the satisfying click when a fine jewelry box snaps shut. It's neat, it's clean, and it's wonderfully tidy. But more than that, when an essay worked, I would know something at the end of those four pages that I didn't know at the beginning. A discovery that I would never have made without fitting those exact words into that tight journalistic sonnet.

My editor said I was free to roam, and roam I did. I wrote about the rejuvenating power of a walk on the beach, about an Indian casino rising obscenely from the pristine Everglades. I wrote a letter to my father who had just passed away, a letter that was more difficult and more vital to me than any piece of writing I'd ever managed. I described trips to the Dry Tortugas and Sanibel and the sleepy town of Saint Petersburg. There are essays about seashells and summer camp and sports teams and Vietnam and car-jacking. I managed finally to write about Hurricane Andrew, which had torn away the solid foundation of our lives. There are essays about the power of books, about libraries, about road rage and the Hardy Boys and my happy memories of wooden tennis rackets. Man, they let me get away with murder.

For three glorious years I had a never-ending reason to pay attention to the Now, to reconsider the long ago, and a powerful incentive to explore the new. But then, one gloomy day, the philistines who ran that paper killed the Sunday magazine and replaced it with an idiotic syndicated version. Since then I have not written a single essay. Which proves my point, I suppose, that hardly anyone voluntarily, without pay or threat of a bad grade, sits down and writes the damn things. But my life is poorer for it. And that came as a great surprise. I miss it. I miss everything about it. Especially that wonderful click at the end.

HOT
DAMN!

HOME AT LAST

Every time I see that bumper sticker—Florida Native—a ripple of envy and irritation flutters in my chest. It's a rare and exotic club to which I will never belong because I'm one of those thousands-a-week folks who have been flooding into Florida for the last few decades. Although they tell us that the tide has slackened to 591 new residents a day, Florida natives are still as scarce and outlandish as manatees. How unfair it seems that even though I've lived in the state for well over thirty years (surely longer than plenty of the younger natives), I should still feel like an interloper.

In 1965 on a south Florida winter day much like this one, I stepped off the train at the Hollywood station to attend Riverside Military Academy. It had been an incredibly romantic journey, a long rumbling train ride through the brown scraggly fields of Tennessee and Georgia, then into the expanse of green nothingness that was north and central Florida, until finally the palm trees began to thicken, the greens grew lush, and the windows in the train slowly lowered. Suddenly I was standing beside the tracks looking at a sky dense with extravagant birds, white and huge with lazy wings, long orange legs trailing.

I remember taking my first breath of rich subtropical air. There was something sweet and spicy in the breeze—that warm macaroon aroma with an intoxicating undertone of cinnamon that seems to waft directly from some secret Caribbean island. That afternoon I breathed in a lungful of air I have yet to release.

Though I didn't have the words for it then, I knew the light was different too. Softer than the harsh and unglamorous Kentucky daylight I was used to. It had an almost romantic, twilight rosiness, a quiet light, yet at the same time far more vivid and precise than any I'd known before. A painterly January light. And while I had been on the platform of the Hollywood train station for less than a minute, I knew with utter certainty that I had taken a mortal wound.

Some time later that winter, I dropped the bombshell on my parents. I informed them that I had decided to turn down the Air Force Academy appointment my father and I had labored so hard to secure. I wanted to attend college in this newly discovered Shangri-la, Florida. While the shock of my passing up a free four years of college must have been incredibly difficult for them to absorb, to their everlasting credit my parents let me win that argument.

I never told them that the institution of higher learning I had chosen, Florida Presbyterian College, had caught my eye because the catalog I'd devoured in my boys' school guidance office had numerous photographs of coeds wearing Bermuda shorts in classrooms. Ah, sweet Florida, what a sensuous and libertine land.

I did four glorious years of college in the charming and soporific Saint Petersburg of the sixties. On holidays I explored the west coast, the Keys, camping at starkly primitive Bahia Honda, building bonfires on midnight beaches, discovering out-of-the-way taverns that served cheap pitchers of beer and spectacular cheeseburgers, bays where fish jumped happily into frying pans, and unair-conditioned piano bars in Key West where writers huddled in the corners and talked the secret talk. I had never felt so at home.

Then I graduated, and after serving a bleak exile in snowy latitudes to collect two more degrees, it was finally time to find a job. I was so determined to return to Florida that I didn't even bother applying for teaching jobs in any other state. It was a cavalier decision bordering on lunacy, for that was a time in the early seventies when teaching jobs were scarce and terminal degrees plentiful. Every taxi driver had one. When no job offer was forthcoming, I moved back to Florida anyway and put my new Ph.D. to use digging holes and planting azaleas, palm trees, and a host of other landscape plants around the bases of high-rise condominiums. Better to do manual labor in the relentless sun of Florida than to find myself in some university office staring out the window at the desolate tundra of *Anyplace Else*.

The phone call finally came. A new state university in Miami. The ground floor. A dream job. And then, little by little, all these years happened. But even after all this time, the light is still new and surreal and the air still drenched with spices they haven't yet named, and the sky is chock-full of the most impossible birds. Parrots squawk across my backyard sky every morning at seven. Garish flowers big as Stetsons bloom in December. Some evenings the breeze is so luxurious I feel like weeping.

I kidnapped a boy from Kentucky and transplanted him in paradise, and he grew up to write books that sing the praises and mock the dizzy and perilous follies of this gaudy corner of the nation. I love this place. I have loved it from the start and have learned to love it more with every passing year—all its quirkiness, its stresses, this simmering melting pot where no one wants to blend.

I have decided we need a bumper sticker of our own—those of us who had the misfortune of being born somewhere else but who made the difficult choices, overcame the fears and complications and the psychic traumas of abandoning the safety of one home for the uncertainty of another. There are 591 stories a day about how we arrived here, and sure, not all of us were as swept away by the sensory treasures of this place as that eighteen-year-old kid on the train platform. Some of us came simply for jobs or to play golf in February or to soothe our arthritic joints, and there are many who find nothing to rhapsodize about in the sumptuous air or rosy light, the awkward, delicious grace of a heron rising into flight. There are many of those 591 who simply ignore or endure what the rest of us cherish. Well, let them get their own license plate. But as for the rest of us, ours should say, Home at Last.

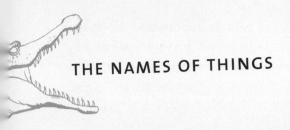

THE NAMES OF THINGS

Lace murex, wentletrap, lightning whelk, junonia. The names are as exotic and various as their shapes. Cones and tulips and angel wings, baby's ears and worms. Their bright colors litter the beach before me and crunch underfoot. With every step down the sugary sand I cringe with guilt at the possibility that I am destroying hundreds of rare specimens.

My wife and I have come for several days of relaxation on Sanibel Island. Each morning at first light we join the hordes who are prowling the shoreline, bent over in what is known in these parts as the *Sanibel stoop*. No one says hello, for all eyes are focused on the wash of new shells that are humped along the high tide mark as my fellow beachcombers inspect this daily bounty with something like the passion of Lotto fever. Some of them are kneeling over thick white beds of shells, sifting through the wreckage with tongue depressors. Some have arrayed their chairs and towels and other gear around their patch of beach while they work with a gold miner's frenzied focus.

Sanibel Island is the best shelling spot in the Western Hemisphere and the third best in the world, ranked just behind Australia and the Philippines. This fourteen-mile-long, shrimp-shaped spit of land is the only one of the barrier islands to run east to west, which makes it a perfect catcher's mitt for shells carried in the Gulf's north-running currents.

Because I'm not normally a beachgoer, these seaside vacations always seem to take a hallowed place in my memory. Dawdling down the sand with no destination and no schedule, we soak up the sensuous beach scene with the purity of Florida newcomers. Everything seems marvelous and strange: the single dolphin rolling near shore, the lapping surf, the hilarious cries of the gulls and the shrieks of toddlers facing their first waves, the ungainly pelicans landing in the high unsteady branches of an Australian pine, a Labrador retriever chasing flock after flock of sandpipers.

To commemorate this rare sunny holiday, I join my fellow beachgoers in prospecting for shells. Since I'm no connoisseur, the only requirement I have for choosing a shell is that it have a special shine when I pluck it from the damp sand. As we walk the shore, we choose and discard, choose and discard, scanning the piles of sculptured jewels at our feet until we spot the perfect specimen, a memento worthy of the day.

A mile or two down the beach, with half a dozen shells in my hand, I see a woman bent over her mound, digging with scrupulous care with what looks like a stainless steel dentist's probe. I show her the handful of shells I've collected so far and ask her if she knows what they are. She studies them for a moment and says no, she's not sure. It is clear that either the shells I've collected are exceedingly rare or this woman is as surprisingly ignorant as I am.

"I guess I should buy a shell book," I say.

"Or just stand in the bookstore and look through one," she offers.

I tell myself that it's not crucially important to know the names of these twisted pieces of calcium. These are, after all, just the carcasses of mollusks, bivalves, gastropods. The slimy things that once inhabited these husks are very far down on my personal hierarchy of compassion. I can't remember the last snail I really cared about.

But there is part of me that wants to know the names of everything. So that afternoon, with our growing cache of shells safely stowed in our room, we head to the Bailey-Matthews Shell Museum in search of enlightenment.

We quickly discover that this is an establishment that takes itself very seriously. Within our first few minutes, we are reminded several times that the Bailey-Matthews Shell Museum is the only museum of its kind in the United States. The high-minded mission statement of the museum is to explain "the miracle of the mollusk" and "the influence of seashells on the affairs of mankind."

My goofiness detector is clicking madly.

But that doesn't last long, for when we enter the Great Hall of Shells we encounter some truly intelligent and sophisticated exhibits on "shells as money," "mollusks, medicine and man," and "shells in architecture." One of the most impressive displays is a series of cameos made of shells, works of folk art as marvelous and eccentric as any I've ever seen. Layers and layers of helmet shells in various shades and colors, arranged in delicate relief images of human faces or landscape portraits.

By the time we leave the museum, I am ready to buy my own stainless steel dental probe and become a full-time prospector. I have learned that mollusks come from eggs, that they are cannibalistic, that the small holes one frequently finds in the empty shells on the beach are drilled by attacking shells, which bore through the shell in order to cut the muscle attaching the mollusk to its armor, so that they can suck out the creamy delicacy inside. I have scribbled down a page of notes, but the one thing I haven't learned is the precise names of the shells that I've so recently collected. They are some kind of whelk, of that I'm fairly sure. But their exact species remains a mystery.

When the vacation is over, we take home our dozen nameless shells and add them to the collection that fills two large glass jars prominently placed in a main thoroughfare of our house, so that we will be reminded continually of a host of beautiful, stress-free days by the Atlantic or the Gulf.

By now my newly acquired shells have lost the glossy, colorful sheen that made me nab them up in the first place and are as dull and bleached out as antique Polaroids. From my recent studies I know that I can lightly coat the shells with oil to revive their vibrancy. But somehow that feels metaphorically wrong. While those languorous Sanibel days and nights, so full of the incense of the sea, are still hauntingly vivid, I know the memories will soon begin to fade, and like the shells, they too will someday be little more than bleached husks. Which is fine. Because then we'll need to replenish them with another trip to the seashore.

FLORIDA TRIFECTA

For nearly thirty years I'd been hearing rousing stories about the quaint inn on Cabbage Key, a mile or so offshore of Sanibel Island. And though I'd been in the vicinity many times and had every intention of exploring the island, something always intervened.

From newspaper articles and word of mouth, I gathered that the island was small and populated with a band of rough-and-tumble eccentrics, modern-day pirates, garrulous fishing guides, and crusty Florida crackers, just my type of characters. Again and again the inn itself had been portrayed in nearly mythic strokes. The walls were said to be papered with thousands of dollar bills, and the ancient mahogany of the bar etched with the names of famous writers. A place that resonated with extraordinary fishing yarns and fabulous tales of old Florida.

But I had delayed my pilgrimage to Cabbage Key for so many years that I had entered the danger zone. Dangerous to go because it was doubtful the reality could live up to the legends, and dangerous to delay for much longer for this was exactly the kind of Florida treasure that every day is being bought up and given a members-only exclusivity. Another offshore bauble snatched away by the million-dollar club.

I decided to risk being disappointed.

I called my friend Randy Wayne White, a fine mystery novelist and columnist for *Outside* magazine. Randy used to be a fishing guide in Fort Myers, and since I had recently taken him dolphin fishing out in the Gulf Stream, leading him to an enormous school of big and active fish, I figured he owed me one. Actually, I figured he owed me two. For shortly after our dolphin expedition, he wrote an article about our day on the water, a scurrilous piece that was published in *Outside* magazine and later reprinted by several unsuspecting newspapers. Let's just say that the article's general subject was seasickness and it reflected badly on me, and ninety-nine percent of the facts in it were unfactual. Randy is, after all, first a fisherman and second a fiction writer, not exactly the credentials to inspire trust in his journalistic probity.

Despite Randy's gross misrepresentations of me, the two of us have remained friends—a credit to my capacity for forgiveness as well as my passionate desire to someday find a way to retaliate for his slanderous article. Although Randy had just that day returned from an exhausting trip to Colombia and other South American territories, he generously invited my wife and me to drop over to see his house on Pine Island and then to take that long-awaited voyage to Cabbage Key.

Like his series hero, Doc Ford, Randy lives a simple life. His old cracker house is tin roofed and has plank floors and looks out at the calm stretch of waters of Pine Island Sound. But best of all, the house backs up on a sixty-acre archaeological preserve, land that the Calusa Indians, a maritime nation of highly skilled sailors, once used for various ceremonial purposes.

As Randy walked us around the hills and plazas of this ancient land, the mystical vibrations were almost palpable, as if enchanted fairy dust still hung in the air. There are so few places in Florida anymore that retain their unbroken connection with the primitive past, that when we stumble onto one of them, there is the sense that we are treading on deeply hallowed ground.

As my psychic tuning fork hummed, we drank a beer together on a peak overlooking one of the assembly plazas and were quieter than we would have been almost anywhere else on earth. I no longer cared if we went over to Cabbage Key. This was fine. We could stay there all afternoon, standing shoulder to shoulder with the ghosts of our noble forebears who knew and loved this land when its waters were crystalline and dense with fish, its breezes uncontaminated by either noise or particulates.

But finally we pulled ourselves away, made the short drive to the tiny marina where Randy keeps his flatboat, and soon we were idling out the channel into Pine Island Sound, although the spell was still on me, a chime tolling deep in the blood, as if I were hearing the haunting echoes of another Florida, a deeper, more mysterious one that forever enchants and eludes us.

As we skimmed across the bay, a pod of dolphins rolled off our bow. The water was sheened with golden sunlight. I was still in my mystical reverie as we pulled into the docks of Useppa Island. Cabbage Key lay a half mile farther out, but Randy thought we should see Useppa first. As we came to learn, the island was developed by the New York advertising mogul Baron Collier, the namesake of Collier County. In the early 1900s Collier built a private mansion on the isolated island as well as a few guest cottages. His guests included Roosevelts, du Ponts, Rothschilds, and Rockefellers, and the afternoon we visited, some of their grandchildren seemed to be lounging there still.

The docks were crammed with great Gibraltars of fiberglass, teak, and chrome. On the hundred acres of land there are a hundred houses with the gray and white lattice, gingerbread, and genteel wood siding of a fabricated Olde Florida. There is a marina, a small restaurant, an inn, and a small museum. There are no roads, only pink shell walkways where golf carts roam. Croquet and tarpon fishing are the main pastimes on the island, aside from a once-a-year parade that the residents throw themselves during the high season when they decorate their golf carts like fruit baskets and racing cars and drive up and down their private beach. Yes, the rich are different from you and me. Goofier.

And then, as the sun was declining, we were on to Cabbage Key. And yes indeed, the walls are papered with dollar bills and the beer is flawlessly cold and the people are eccentric and polite and love to unspool their yarns. And the aura of mystery novelist and playwright Mary Roberts Rinehart still hovers above the charming inn that she helped design as a private residence some sixty years ago.

There was a wedding the night we arrived, and because we were Randy's friends we were heartily welcomed to the party and invited to help excavate an enormous hill of fresh boiled shrimp. The piano player was enjoying himself, the newlyweds glowed, there was dancing, there was song, there were bawdy jokes and strong drink. We taped our autographed dollar to the thousands already there. The perfect end to a perfect Florida trifecta, a day of Indians, millionaires, and crackers—that three-pronged platform on which we modern Floridians stand.

And suddenly my wish to find some way to skewer Randy White seemed cheap and small, withering in my breast like the last shreds of daylight on the distant horizon.

NUDE WOMAN IN THE GRASS

My love affair with books began as most serious romances do, when I was least expecting to fall in love. I was ten years old, maybe eleven, and for years I had dutifully read the required books in school, but because they were required and because I was tested on my comprehension of them, I had decided that reading books ranked alongside long division and penmanship as simply one more bothersome educational duty.

Context is important here, for I was a young male in a southern town of the 1950s. In other words, that I would read a book just for fun was about as likely as my deciding spontaneously to knit a sweater for the football coach. It wasn't done. At least not by any of the male role models who shaped my thinking at the time.

So when my mother deposited me at the public library that fall afternoon to get me out of her hair while she went about her downtown errands, she might as well have dropped me off in the middle of Death Valley. The gloomy building was one of those

WPA structures built in the heavily ornate style of the Old South. That creaky battleship was piloted by a wispy, white-haired woman in a dark dress and thick glasses, a living cliché who floated noiselessly up and down the stacks replacing volumes in their proper slots and leaving the dry dust of tedium in her wake. As a young boy who aspired only to muscular achievements on hash-marked fields or gymnasium floors, I was mortified. Frightened out of my skin that I would be spotted by one of my friends in such a place.

To make myself as invisible as possible I moseyed down aisle after aisle studying the titles of those musty tomes, bored to death by the prospect of spending an hour or two in that dismal room. When the passing librarian seemed to sense my discomfort and began to home in on me, a fit of panic spurred me to nab a random book from a shelf, pop it open to the first page, and feign deep interest.

As my eyes ran down the lines of print, I was suddenly breathless. Though my vocabulary was no larger than that of any average ten-year-old boy of my place and time, I did know the word *nude*. It was one of those special, cherished words, not quite a curse, but nonetheless a word loaded with magical potency. And lo and behold that very word leaped out of the first page and seized my full attention. The fact that the word *nude* turned out to be an adjective modifying the word *woman* made my knees weak and put a wobble in my pulse.

I looked up, certain that the librarian was about to rip this smutty book from my hand, grab me by the collar, and toss me onto the street. By evening it would be all over town: "Little Jimmy Hall was caught reading that nude woman book in the library." But magically, the librarian melted back into the stacks, and I was left alone with my first murder mystery novel.

For the nude woman was dead, and it was her corpse that had been found in a field by a man chasing butterflies. How did she get there? Who was she? Who would have done such a thing? I was mesmerized. Weak of breath and nearly fainting from a pre-adolescent tumult of emotions, I located a private corner near a window. I looked around and planned my getaway should my mother suddenly reappear and find me reading that filth. Then I sped through as many pages as I could manage before she returned and called me away.

To my disappointment, there was no graphic description of the woman's nudity, nor was there any further mention of her appearance in the tall grasses of that field. Nevertheless, I was hooked on the story— the exact condition its author must have hoped to inspire.

So this was why people read! Books were about adult things. Strong emotions, extreme behaviors, the inside stuff of a world I had never imagined existed. In this my first recreational book I suddenly realized that novels could fill one with heart-pounding fear as well as lip-smacking lust. That they could, in fact, suddenly expand the boundaries of the tiny hillbilly town where I had always lived and where I imagined I would always stay.

Tramping across the bogs of the English countryside in pursuit of the heinous killer of that nude woman, I was suddenly freed of my homebound life. I was set loose in the world and allowed to know every crucial thought of that droll British detective and was just as stumped as he, just as frustrated, and finally just as delighted when the logic of his deductions led him to the surprising culprit.

It took me several more surreptitious visits to the library to finish that novel. Surely my mother and father were deeply puzzled by this new enthusiasm, but they had the good grace not to ask where it was coming from. That might have quashed it all.

The day I finished that first novel, I looked up to find the amiable librarian staring down at me.

I gulped.

"You like mysteries?" she asked.

I gazed at the book in my hand as though it had just materialized there.

"Oh, this?"

"Yes, that. That book you've been reading these last few weeks."

"I guess so," I said.

"Well, so do I." She beamed. "I just love a good murder story." And she gave me a conspiratorial look that still floats into my mind whenever I am feeling isolated from the human race. For as I have come to understand, reading is at once a private and a communal act. While books are savored alone, they grant you membership in the most fascinating club I know: fellow readers. Fellow voyagers into the vast uncharted waters of imaginative literature.

That afternoon the librarian gave me a private tour of that big dusty room and showed me the best mysteries in the house. Hard-boiled, cozies, Sherlock Holmes. She made a pile, got me a library card, helped me fill it out.

"Tell me what you think," she said.

"Okay," I said uncertainly.

"Oh, don't worry, this isn't school," she said. "There's no test when you bring them back. I won't take your library card away from you if you don't read one all the way through."

"I don't know," I said. "I don't know if I'm smart enough to read all these." I patted the stack of books.

"Oh, my," she said. "No one starts out smart. That's why we read."

Over the next few years I gradually climbed onto the literary high road and read Dickens and Hardy and Joyce, and later I fell in love with Lawrence Durrell and John Fowles, Faulkner and Steinbeck, and the poets Sylvia Plath and Anne Sexton and Robert Frost. It came as a shock to learn that sports and reading were not mutually exclusive. In fact, when I discovered Hemingway and began reading about his intense competitive exploits, I started to picture the unspeakable—that I might someday learn the craft of writing well enough to create the very things I so dearly loved to consume.

Though that creaky library no longer exists in my small Kentucky hometown, and though I have fled her narrow streets and scrubby fields forever, the largest part of what I am today and what I know about the world and about the affairs of the human heart springs from that one autumn afternoon when I plucked a book from the shelf and encountered that nude woman lying in the grass and I began this long journey, year after year, filling myself beyond the brim with the great accumulated wealth of books.

BACK TO SCHOOL

Here we are again, the end of something, the beginning of something else. That strange, ambiguous swirl of regret and high expectations that rises in the heart the first of each September. Summer vacation is over, and it's time to start making new resolutions, summoning a fresh burst of energy and purpose. Time to buy a new pencil box, a new wardrobe, new books, new notebook and papers and pens. The school year has begun.

For the last forty-six years I've been measuring my year by semesters. Since that morning my mother led me past the iron gates of Virginia Street Elementary and left me behind in a cramped wooden desk with a hole cut out for an inkwell, I have been living by the rhythms and holidays and strange circadian cycles of school. Perpetually caught in a fiscal year a delicious three months shorter than the one almost everyone else lives by.

If someone had told me on that morning forty-six years ago that I would spend the rest of my adult life in school, I would have run screaming into the dark woods and joined a band of feral children. Who in their right mind would want to forever endure the regimented rows of chairs, the daunting chalkboard that stretched across the entire front of the room, the ceaseless fluorescent lights, the tedious repetition of multiplication tables, and the grueling hours practicing penmanship? As that list suggests, school has long been a model of industrial training, teaching at least as much about the assembly line as about academic subjects. Why I would ever have wanted to become an educational shop foreman for the rest of my days is utterly incomprehensible.

Certainly I had few inspirational teaching models to lure me into this career. In the second grade, for instance, there was Miss Gene McKee, a portly lady of unfathomable age who had also been my parents' second grade teacher, a fact that I still find stunning. One of Miss McKee's more memorable traits was to prowl the room looking for wayward feet that had wandered out from under the desks and were resting vulnerable in the aisle. Approaching from the rear, the ponderous Miss McKee would step on our virginal toes, grind her heel against them, and bear down with her entire two hundred plus pounds. If she found no feet to trample, other parts of the anatomy would do just as well. A fidgeting hand might get a crack from the ruler across the knuckles, and a whisper to a classmate sometimes earned a forceful whack with the same ruler across the back of the offender's head.

Sometimes I wish such martial arts were still allowed. A nice toe mash might be just the thing to arouse those somnolent students who come straight from an eight-hour workday to slump in the front row of my class and execute their fluttering lip snores. And a well-placed ruler could be just the tool I've been looking for to convince that occasional pupil suffering from terminal smugness that, yes, even someone as gifted as he might still require the meager services of an educational mentor.

There is at the beginning of this new school year, as in every seasonal cycle, a great sense of hope and determination. This year I will get it right. This semester I will fulfill my highest teaching aspirations. Day after day, the room will resonate with scholarly exhilaration. All the challenges I present to my students will be met and surpassed. They will be stimulated to heights of learning they previously considered themselves incapable of. Because of my inspirational teaching they will all reach a crucial watershed moment of understanding, after which they will be better, wiser, more productive human beings.

Even though I have so far failed to realize most of these dreams, I remain hopeful. For there is embedded in the academic process the secret, unexpressed belief that these books, these tests, these lectures and discussions will add up to some changed condition, an enrichment of the soul, an enlargement of the sense of human possibilities. Perhaps it is this very fact, that the goals of a teacher are loftier than the aims of most ordinary workers, that lured me into teaching to begin with. For like most teachers, a dogged sense of idealism drives me. We teachers are not simply trying to make a better widget, or sell a better product, or design a better mousetrap. We are trying to re-create the world. Enlarge the possibilities of our fellow beings. We are suckers for optimism just as we are missionaries for our subject area. We English professors are simply brimming over with zeal for a well-groomed sentence, an innovative thought, a subtle argument, and a coherent, well-oiled essay.

But even though I feel the old excitement begin to build again this week as I compose the semester's syllabus, imagining each of those upcoming classes, still, something in me quietly rebels. For although I have spent nearly thirty years in the south Florida climate, I have not completely adjusted. Some archetypal instinct revolts against going back to the classroom in the midst of all this heat and humidity. Where are the autumn colors? Where is the hint of smoke wafting up from burning piles of leaves? Where is that old favorite sweater scented with mothballs, dragged out of the chest of drawers to wear on the first cool evening of fall?

Fall semester is its name, but in south Florida that's a terrible misnomer. Miss Gene McKee wouldn't believe it for a second. She'd still be drowsing on her front porch on Main Street, dreaming of toes inching into the aisle. Imagining those squirming hands, those whispering lips. She would not rouse herself to go back to the classroom in such everlasting heat. If Miss Gene were teaching in south Florida, she might have to wait almost till Christmas before she caught that first whiff of autumn in the air.

But alas, the calendar says that summer is over, even when my senses tell me otherwise. And I must somehow rekindle those hopeful visions, fire up the neurons again, buy a couple of new shirts, a new note-book, some fresh pens, and with one final parting glance at the three months I've spent in happy indo-lence, I head again toward the old iron gates where my mother led me so many years ago.

WINNING ME OVER

To celebrate the fiftieth anniversary of the opening of Everglades National Park, I decided to drive out into that stark and endless prairie and take in the sights. It was nearly a quarter of a century ago that I first journeyed west out Tamiami Trail and fell instantly in love with that broad and watery expanse of sawgrass and anhingas and alligators. What struck me on that first trip was the way the vast and mesmerizing distances seemed to open up immediately after passing beyond the city limits of Miami. At that time I did not yet know the name of a single bird or bush or tree, and my eyes were not yet attuned to the nuances of that profoundly understated landscape, yet I sensed the aching silence, a mysterious, almost sacred hush that seemed to resonate from the immense spread of sky and land.

Twenty-five years later that magical resonance is still there. But now there is another sound. Not the roar of bulldozers, or the ceaseless grind of asphalt pavers, not the *whack, whack* of more cookie-cutter suburbs being flung up as we relentlessly nibble at the Everglades, bleed away its sweet, secret waters.

No, now there are new noises out in that river of grass, sounds that have never been heard in this land before. There are chimes and toots and synthetic ricochets, the *ka-ching, ka-ching* of some synthesized cash register, and high above that electronic din there comes a loud and frantic human cry—a woman's voice calling out, "Bingo! Bingo!"

I have come to visit the Miccosukee Indian Gaming Casino.

The building rises out of the pristine waters on a hump of gray fill, an aggressively ugly structure, the kind of huge square corrugated monstrosity that one might expect in an industrial park somewhere around the airport. A place where bowling balls might be manufactured or perhaps some obscure plumbing fixture. At ten o'clock on a weekday morning, the parking lot is half full.

It is one of those faultless south Florida days, twenty-four hours after the latest front has passed through. The sky scrubbed back to its crystalline blue, a cool breeze sliding down the state spiced with Canadian evergreen. The light is as sharp and true as any I've ever seen. It is a perfect day to ride a bike out the path at Shark Valley and count deer and alligators and great blue herons. But I'm on a different mission today, so I forge on past the signs warning of Live Alligators and push through the smoky glass doors into the airless gloom of the casino.

I stand there a moment gathering myself, recovering from the shocking transition. I'm reflecting on those alligator signs, wondering if perhaps they are meant to be ironic, or if the Miccosukees are simply following their lawyers' advice to avoid liability suits. I can't say I've heard of any luckless gambler being attacked by an alligator in the casino parking lot, but then a lot of events that I would consider relevant news stories never make it into the paper. Perhaps the signs are simply meant as a general admonition: Abandon Hope All Ye Who Enter Here. If the gators don't get you, the Lotto machine will.

I take a moment to jot down one or two of these thoughts and am immediately confronted by a security guard with a state trooper's hat and a large gun and a shirt that is shrink-wrapped over his Schwarzenegger body.

"What're you writing?" he asks me.

"I'm just taking down a few notes."

"Why?"

"I'm writing an article," I say, "For the newspaper."

"Let me see your press pass."

Months ago, I had asked for a press pass, but my request was met with gentle derision. After all, I was told, these columns hardly require me to elbow my way to the front of a growling pack of real reporters.

"You're a journalist, but you don't have a press pass?" The security guard allows himself the slightest sarcasm.

I go on the attack.

"What's the big deal? What're you worried about? I'm just writing down a few thoughts."

He demands to see my notes, snaps them out of my hand, and tells me to wait right there while another security guard at least as brutish as the first steps in to guard me. A few minutes later an even more humorless young man appears with my notes. At least this one isn't wearing a gun. The young man is squinting at my scribbling as if he were trying to decode hieroglyphics. Coming close, he looks me over, looks again at the notes. He isn't much impressed with either.

Maybe I am going to take that bike ride out through Shark Valley after all. Or maybe these guys were going to haul me off to their own private hideaway in the Glades, a place set aside for guys like me with the audacity to take notes in the casino. It suddenly occurs to me that these guys are what the signs outside were warning me about.

This young man hands me back my pad and tells me I am free to stay in the casino, but I can take no more notes, I cannot write down the numbers of any of the machines, and I cannot interview any of the employees. I may play the machines, or I may go. Though I am deeply disappointed the manager has found nothing in my notes sufficiently incisive to warrant kicking me out, I decide to stay.

I've never been much of a gambler. Once when researching a novel I took a cruise to the Bahamas, and on the first night I won nine hundred dollars on the slot machines. I put the nine hundred in my wallet and hung out on the upper deck the rest of the cruise. Luck is luck, that's all it is. It means nothing. You can't court it, you can't ride it, you can't run out of it. It's stray particles firing out of the universe, bombarding each of us randomly. Nothing we can control. But still, I give the forty dollars I've brought along my super secret lucky rub and proceed down the aisles.

Normally I like slot machines. Cranking the levers allows you to pretend you're working, not just trying to get something for nothing. And with a lever in your hand you get that satisfying gear mesh of good machinery, and if you try real hard, you can imagine you're having some minor effect on the outcome of the whirling numbers. But the Miccosukees have high-tech machines. You touch the cold glass of the screen, and the computer reads your finger's presence, and a little electronic dance occurs that simulates a mechanical slot machine. It's very cold and dispassionate. It's very empty. It's very much like the eyes of the security guard and the manager, who were no doubt watching me through their video cameras to make sure I wasn't jotting any of these thoughts down.

Instead of cherries and oranges in the slot machines, the Miccosukees have opted for images of peace pipes, Indians in headdresses, bows and arrows, arrowheads, and eagles. Generic Native American stuff, not very politically correct, but I suppose they can get away with parodying themselves. These stereotypes certainly are not arousing the ire of any of the zombies around me. Their mouths hang slightly ajar as they touch the screen and touch the screen again and touch and touch and touch.

In the midst of the casino there is a small café where the headings on the menu are Jackpot of Soups, Lucky Starters, High Roller Specials, Side Bets, and Other Good Bets. At least somebody has a sense of humor. There are traditional Miccosukee jackets for sale at a gift shop. Distributed all around the floor are replicas of hollowed-out logs that are used as ashtrays. Other than that, I see nothing that would remind a gambler he was in the center of the most magical and most endangered national park in America.

Down to my last five dollars and ready to leave, I win a jackpot. It is enough to pay the mortgage this month and buy all my Christmas presents. It is a lot more than I won on the cruise ship. After the attendant gives me my money, I hold it up for the security cameras to see, and I march to the exit. If they were trying to buy me off so I'd write a positive story about their wretched casino, they underestimated me.

They don't have a jackpot big enough for that.

DREAM HOUSE

A little over six years ago, my wife and I decided it was time to move from the home I'd bought during my bachelor days. When I'd purchased that house in Miami Shores, I'd been nurturing a fantasy about boating to work. So I'd located a home on a canal that was close enough to the waterfront university to make such a journey feasible, and I did, in fact, boat to work off and on for a couple of years. But the allure of the fantasy gradually waned, and we came to see that no matter what remodeling projects we undertook on the place in Miami Shores, the structure was far too prosaic to ever become our dream house.

For despite much evidence to the contrary, we still believed that it was possible to find a house in south Florida a few degrees closer to our ideal, that idyllic Wordsworthian cottage in the woods that both of us had been yearning for all our lives.

For months we combed Miami, searching for the exact blend of character and land that defined that dream house, a misty image that seemed to lurk just beyond the borders of consciousness. During that time we stopped at so many open houses in Coral Gables, South Miami, and Coconut Grove and visited so many others with Realtors that even now, years later, it is hard for us to drive anywhere in south Florida without bumping into one of those places that we explored and rejected. There are even several houses that we returned to three or four times and were on the verge of buying, and it is those houses that now give us shivers, for we realize how close we came to settling for something less than our dream.

We saw plenty of homes in the Grove and Gables and other parts of south Florida that had appealing characteristics. Old houses with thick stucco walls and balconies and barrel tile roofs, or shady Grove homes on serpentine streets that reeked of charm. But inevitably those houses were built on cramped lots with bedroom windows staring forever into the neighbor's bedroom window. While a few miles south of Miami we found the lots to be larger, almost all the homes out there were constructed in the fifties and sixties and for the most part had the elegance and grace of strip shopping malls.

It was in the spring of 1992 when we finally stumbled into our future. We had spent yet another tiring day with a Realtor touring bland neighborhoods with interchangeable homes. We were worn down by the unceasing parade of rejects, and on the verge of abandoning the quest entirely. Evelyn was in the backseat studying the Multiple Listing Service printout sheets, all the places within our price range in that part of town. As the day was winding down, she spotted a listing that sounded intriguing. What caught her eye was the word *outbuilding*.

From the beginning, my image of a dream house had included a building separate from the main house, a place where my office could be safely placed beyond the range of humdrum duties and responsibilities. A world apart.

The house that Evelyn spotted had not one but two outbuildings. We were doubly intrigued. So the Realtor called, set up an appointment, and the house became the last one we looked at that day. Indeed, it ended our house shopping in south Florida forever.

Now, I was no real estate neophyte. I am the son of a real estate broker, and I had at that time bought and sold several houses. I knew full well who our Realtor worked for and that we were in effect consorting with the adversary. Nevertheless, as we drove through the front gates onto the property of that final house, I blurted out, "Oh, my god, this is it. I don't care what it costs. This is it." By the time I got control of myself, the damage was done. I am certain that for the next thirty years we will be paying several hundred extra dollars a month for that outburst.

The house was wooden, with clapboard siding of Dade County pine. A farmhouse with a full screened-in front porch, double-hung windows, and a high peaked tin roof. Wings of the house meandered off in different directions, a graceful maze. That day we first saw it, it was painted white, and the paint was blistering off the house in great flakes. But that didn't matter. And neither did the fact that both the outbuildings were tiny. One was a barn barely large enough for a single horse; the other was the pump house where the irrigation equipment for the avocado grove once resided. The house, we came to discover, was built originally by the caretaker of the avocado grove that spread for acres around this part of town.

There was a small swimming pool with a waterfall, a white gazebo poised next to it. The house was positioned on the acre and a half so that it gazed into the depths of the property, turning its side to the quiet street and the rest of the neighborhood. The neighboring homes were distant and invisible behind the lush vegetation. At that season of the year the avocado trees were shedding their leaves and the yard was full of their crackling music. There was cool shade everywhere, a high white privacy fence that blocked the narrow street from view, and on the other side was a forest of enormous Australian pines moaning in the breeze. Trees everywhere, avocados and mangoes, oaks and rosewoods, orange and lime, and a scattering of palms. Birds dancing in the branches.

All this was a blur as we walked into the long screened-in front porch and through a set of French doors into the living room with a soaring cathedral ceiling. We were throbbing with excitement, shooting each other looks. This is it, this is it, this is it.

The house was full of cages. Possums and owls and screeching parrots. The wife ran an animal rehab hospital from her home. But the menagerie only added to the charm. The husband was an FBI prosecutor who specialized in drug cases. A man whose justifiable paranoia had caused him to cut a hobbit door into the back of his bedroom closet. This escape hatch opened through an adjoining wall into what was once the garage, so that when the cocaine cowboys inevitably stormed the front door, the husband and wife could bail out through their secret exit. A perfect south Florida amenity.

The room that became my study was off in a wing by itself, not detached but far enough from the house to promote that illusion. Pecky cypress walls, high wood-beamed ceiling. The FBI guy had barricaded the windows of my office with heavy bookshelves, so that when we first saw it, the room was as gloomy as a midnight bunker. But behind those shelves we discovered beautiful arched windows that now give me a spacious view of the front drive and backyard and fill my study with glorious light.

Not trusting our own inflamed senses that first day, we called some close friends, who drove over to provide a second opinion. "It's gorgeous. You're going to love it," she said. "It's high maintenance," he observed. And now, after living here for five years, I see how prophetic they both were.

I have unintentionally memorized my contractor's beeper number. I know plumbers and electricians and tile guys and painters and wallpapers by their first names. We spent the first six months we lived in the house repairing every cranny of the place. And then Hurricane Andrew tore through the neighborhood, and we spent the next six months doing it all again.

The storm took all but one of our mangoes and obliterated our pine forest and cut our avocados in half. But it taught us a great deal about the flexibility and sturdiness of that old wooden structure, and now, almost five years later, in this wonderful petri dish we call south Florida, the canopy is as dense as it was that first day, the bougainvillea even more luxuriant.

By now we have buried two dogs here, raised two more from puppies. We have planted dozens of trees and rosebushes, and I've written several novels in the prosecutor's former foxhole. It is such a perfect fit that sometimes it feels as if we were born in this house, have lived here several lifetimes.

Our house might be fifty years old, or seventy. We aren't sure. And there's little to compare it to. Out in this part of town, most of the old wooden homes have long ago been bulldozed and replaced by ten thousand square feet of cement block charm. By real estate standards, there is nothing in the area that is considered comparable. An appraiser's nightmare. In fact, on the tax rolls our house is listed as virtually worthless. The land is what we're billed for.

We find that wonderfully ironic. For after living here for years, the unceasing restlessness we used to feel has finally vanished. We are soothed by this house in ways that are almost mystical, and we feel as deeply rooted to this piece of earth as are the trees. It seems only fitting for this place to be beyond appraisal.

TWO HOMES

At seventeen I made my escape from Hopkinsville, Kentucky, the small hillbilly community where I'd grown up. I felt trapped. Stranded in a world of narrow-mindedness and conformity. No future there for a kid with big dreams. I couldn't wait to flee to a place like south Florida, a land I imagined to be rich in possibilities and sophistication.

What I did not know at seventeen was something I am only just now coming to fully understand. No matter how far I was to roam, no matter how much I would change, transcending the limitations of that sleepy two-stoplight town of my youth, it would not be possible to completely escape it as long as my parents were still alive and as long as they chose to live in that same place where they were raised and they raised me. Indeed, no matter how much I may want to believe that south Florida is my home, I am a man with two homes.

For most of the thirty-plus years I've been away, I've done my part to keep the umbilical intact with regular phone calls and less regular letters. On the phone my parents have always acted out their consistent personalities. My mother does most of the talking, while my father, on their second phone, listens, speaking only when he is spoken to. Sometimes after several minutes on the phone listening to my mother chatter on, I've had to ask, "Is Dad there?" "Yep, right here," he says.

Carrying on a relationship over the phone is invariably difficult, but when one of the parties (in this case my mother) is always in a rush to hang up from the moment the hellos are exchanged, conversations can have the hurried quality of last-second partings as the train is pulling out of the station. I know my mother is frugal, another of her Depression-era habits that never faded. And though I remind her that with the current long-distance rates as low as they are, we can talk for an entire three minutes for what it would cost to mail a single letter, nothing I say seems to relax her. Even if I'm the one who's calling, the clock is always hammering in the background.

Our letters back and forth have been so sporadic that they have never fulfilled the role of true dialogue. We all write only when the spirit moves us, and with months between the letters, it is not possible to remember, much less respond to, the other's previous epistle. So every letter has more of the quality of a diary entry, a song to oneself, rather than a true communication. Nevertheless, the day a letter from home arrives is a special day. Not just for the news it brings, but for all the charming idiosyncrasies that are conveyed in the styles of the letters.

For as long as I remember, my mother's letters have

been littered with underlined words and exclamation points. Some words or phrases are underlined once, some twice, and some rate three underlines. She is as emphatic in her letter writing as she is in person. A woman full of energy and opinions, which she is determined to make known.

My father's letter writing was far less frequent than my mother's. Partly because of that, and partly because his were always full of natural descriptions of the weather, the changing seasons, the trees and flowers and birds, his letters seem more dear. Though my mother's penmanship was always graceful, it seemed a bit more schoolgirlish and conventional than my father's ornate handwriting. His script always had a flair, a quiet flamboyance that was curiously at odds with his own subdued demeanor. As though in that elegant script he was allowing himself to exercise an otherwise repressed artistic temperament.

After my father retired from the real estate business some fifteen years ago, he took a course in the local community college where he studied, and quickly mastered, the art of calligraphy. Suddenly his handwriting was full of these ornate flourishes, and his letters turned into small works of art, as beautiful to behold as they were interesting to read. The delicacy and care that he obviously exercised in writing a letter was stunning. Full of inky arabesques, these letters lie like small glowing treasures in one of my desk drawers.

A couple of years ago, I gave my dad a laptop computer. Since my brother and I had spoken often about the marvels of computer technology and my dad always seemed fascinated by the conversations, I thought he might find it fun to play around with one. In no time this seventy-five-year-old man was surfing the Internet. And suddenly I was received e-mails from him. These notes had the same hurried, telegraphic quality of most e-mail communication. Slightly more thought out than a casual phone conversation but not quite as formal as a regular letter, e-mails seem to have a formula all their own. They are disposable communication, notes dashed off and flung as casually as paper airplanes into the electronic abyss. Less weighty than letters, quicker, without great concern for punctuation or spelling, these communications seem uniquely appropriate to our hurried modern time.

In one of his earliest e-mails, sent to all family members in his address book, my father seemed to be as astonished as the rest of us were with his quick mastery of this technology. "For someone who started out with a handcrank telephone," he wrote, "this is all pretty magical."

One of the positive features of e-mail, which affected my dad just as it seems to have affected millions of others, is that it loosens the tongue. In the months after he got on-line I received more e-mail notes from him than I had ever received normal letters. I answered everything. And suddenly the reticence that had always existed between us seemed to be deteriorating. In these private, intimate, instantaneous exchanges we were carrying on the dialogue that had eluded us before.

Though the volume of communication between us has increased, I still miss the calligraphy. I miss the beautiful, sculpted creations that he painted on fine bond paper. Printing out his e-mail with its routing address and its Internet gobbledygook is clearly a diminished thing. But because I've chosen to live a two days' drive from my other home, I'm not in a position to be choosy. I am thankful for any word at all about the lives of these people I love. If that word is filtered through silicon and fiber optics before it is digitally re-created on my computer screen, then so be it. It's simply one of the prices I must pay to live in two places at once.

THE HARDY BOYS

The palest ink is better than the best memory.
—CHINESE PROVERB

It's exhausting to try to recall events from forty years ago. No matter how hard I try, the past remains a slippery, unreliable place, difficult to conjure up, especially with the faulty synapses of middle age. At best I can bring back quick video snippets of this or that moment when I was ten years old. Playing with my rubber army men in the sandbox, gluing together model cars in the basement. The traumatic events, few as they were, are far more vivid. That afternoon our dog was hit by a car and dragged itself into a drainage pipe at the end of our long driveway. And I was elected to crawl into that narrow pipe to haul the half-dead, snapping dog out into the light.

The town where I grew up has changed dramatically. So has my boyhood house. The grade school my parents attended and where I followed decades later no longer exists. It was bulldozed years ago. The bricks and mortar were hauled away, the oak floors and tall windows and musty cloakrooms lie rotting in the landfill of history. In some ways, that makes revisiting those places easier, because there are no messy contradictions between memory and present-tense reality.

One of my most precise memories from forty years ago is that of stretching out on my bed, the pillow wedged against the wall, a book of fiction spread open on my belly. No doubt I spent more hours in my youth playing sports than I did reading. But it is the reading I remember now with exquisite clarity. Not the books themselves, though some of them are still clear, but the act of reading itself is what I most remember. The quiet, inward hours when I was transported from those Kentucky hills, enjoying the secret thrills of my first encounters with danger, heroism, romantic love, sin and redemption, and a hundred other adult emotions that I had yet to face in real experience.

I would like to claim that I was immediately drawn to the kind of book that I now teach, literary novels of depth and scope and complexity. Dickens or Hardy or Brontë. And yes, it's true, I did read those authors eventually, and came to love them too, but at ten or eleven what addicted me to a lifelong habit of reading was nothing so lofty as Thomas Hardy, but rather a series of adventure stories written by Franklin W. Dixon that featured two brothers, one fifteen years old and one sixteen. Their names were Frank and Joe. The Hardy Boys.

Recently, I decided to take another look at these heroes of my youth. Sure I would be disappointed, I set aside the two or three other books I was reading at the moment and took down from the shelves an ancient copy of *The Missing Chums*.

On the cover of the book is what appears to be a rendering of an oil painting. The Hardy Boys are posed together in the cockpit of a wooden speedboat. It is nighttime, and they are steering their boat through a stormy sea, their spotlight illuminating another boat in the distance. The boys are dressed in sweaters and caps and heavy trousers, clothes so classic they might be found in the latest Eddie Bauer catalog. Though this book was published over seventy years ago, there's an eerie timelessness about these two kids, from their clothes to their haircuts. These boys who were once my idols, mature teenage young men, could now easily be my sons.

I cracked open the book and stepped into that time-warp world.

The boys' father, Fenton Hardy, is a detective, and in this adventure he has left the boys and their long-suffering mother to go off to Chicago in pursuit of a very dangerous bad guy named Baldy Turk. Shortly after he's gone, two of the Hardy Boys' closest chums, Chet Morton and Biff Hooper, set out on a boating trip and promptly disappear. It is up to the Hardy Boys to find them.

In addition to their speedboat, Frank and Joe Hardy both owned motorcycles. They were upper-class kids, one of many things I had forgotten about them. But there's nothing namby-pamby about these two. In the next two hundred pages they steer their craft expertly through a vicious storm, bravely board a suspicious sailing ship on a pitch-dark night, and are chased overboard with guns blazing behind them. They explore an island that's slithering with dangerous snakes, and they fight hand to hand against a group of rogues and rascals who have captured their friends and are holding them hostage. They are chained together in a dank cave yet somehow manage to break free of their metal handcuffs and outwit their guards. Finally, they execute an ingenious plan to trap their captors on the island of lethal snakes, hauling away the bad guys' boats and leaving them stranded until the Hardy Boys can bring back adult reinforcements.

An hour or two in that ageless world and I was feeling again the pulse-quickening excitement of long ago and an admiration for these two resourceful brothers, their good sense, their mannerly bravery.

But there was something else beyond the story that was working on me while I lay with that book open on my chest. Some whiff of that long-departed time with its innocence and yearning. I wasn't simply reading a book I'd read forty years ago. I was reading a book then and now, simultaneously in both those times at once.

Experts tell us that of all the senses, it is the sense of smell that has the greatest power to stir the memory. And surely that is partly why I felt myself suddenly straddling the forty-year divide: the musty scent of that book. Its dry, crumbling texture was filling the air with a halo of particles, clones of the particles I had inhaled while reading the book almost half a century before. The experience was so startling, so utterly out-of-body that I had to set the book aside and remind myself of where I was and who I had become.

By the end of the novel, the missing chums were missing no more and the Hardy Boys had once more earned their names. And I was reminded again of the magical, transforming power of books, their ability to transport us beyond our puny lives and to shape the very texture of our personalities. But unlike so many other formative influences in our lives, books don't change over the years. No wrecking ball or bulldozer can demolish their place in the world. They lie waiting for us, constant, neatly arranged on the shelves, all their marvels intact, their stories and characters as supple and energetic as they were forty years ago. A voice that stirred us once, whispered dreams to our younger selves, is still there waiting, ready to whisper once again.

IT'S NOT THE HEAT, IT'S THE STUPIDITY

The poincianas are blooming again, the golden shower trees are raining petals, the avocados dangle like hundreds of small green thumbs from every branch, hitching a ride into summer. Along the fences bougainvillea clusters put a purple flutter in the air. Everywhere the barren twigs are thickening with foliage, and the butterflies begin their brief, exquisitely goofy flight patterns.

For weeks the joggers on my street who gather at six-thirty each morning have watched the subtle signs and have known that any morning now we would wake to find that overnight the air had become nearly unbreathable, so soaked with humidity it was more fit for gills than lungs. We have been sniffing the air for weeks, seeking out those last pockets of cool air, knowing that our brief fling with what is known as winter was nearly done.

Then one morning recently it happened. Because we huff along the same route almost every day and stop and chat at the end of the run, we have become intimately familiar with the unique sweat patterns our group produces. (I shudder to admit that I bring forth on the front of my T-shirt a sweaty replica of Mickey Mouse.) But on this day we looked around and the evidence was clear. Everyone was soaked. Not a dry thread anywhere. So there it was, long before the official date of its arrival, summer had snapped shut around us like an airless casket.

Of course, there are those hairsplitters who might quibble with me, but in my opinion, we have only two seasons in south Florida, summer and not-quite-summer. My guess is that not-quite-summer lasts approximately thirty days. Those thirty exquisite, crystalline days are sprinkled over the four months of tourist season, a period when we must share our region with a few million freeloaders who have not paid their summer dues. For four months those cheaters crowd our streets and interstates, form lines outside our best restaurants, throng to the beaches and bays, and suck down gallons of our luscious air. And when they've got their tan and eaten their fill of lobster, they head home just in time to miss the suffocating advent of summer.

Well, good riddance. Even if it does mean that not-quite-summer is over, I'm glad they're gone. As they say in Minnesota (using distinctly different numbers), "Ninety degrees and ninety percent humidity keeps the riffraff out." For the next eight months we have this place to ourselves again, and though I no longer count myself among those who actually relish the heat, I at least look forward to this time of year so I can begin to renew my acquaintance with some of the places that until Easter were too crowded to enjoy.

For most of my life I *did* love the heat. I spent nearly every summer day of my youth at the local pool and was brown as a coffee bean before the summer was over. Remember when we thought the sun was good for you? All that vitamin A and D? Well, I soaked up tons of A and D for most of thirty years. I was a lifeguard at the college pool, a member of the tennis team, playing shirtless for hours every afternoon in the Florida sun, and later I worked construction for a year or so, bare-backed and without a hat, bleaching my brown hair to a shrill blond. I tanned easily and was proud of the fact, and there simply wasn't a day too hot for me.

I suppose some of the psychic resonance I feel about summer heat is left over from my long days of imprisonment in public schools. Like so many of us who grew up in northern climes, I spent a great deal of my school year staring out the window at a stark winter landscape, yearning for summer. And when that last bell rang and I raced out into fields and lakes to bask in the golden swelter, I thought of heat as my reward, as the great, glorious payoff for all I'd suffered in that gloomy, interminable winter.

Though I have only anecdotal evidence from a few native Floridians, it appears to me that those who grew up in south Florida are not as deeply imprinted with the positives of summer as those of us from the north. But these days I have to thank god that I do have those favorable recollections of summer, for I find myself calling more and more on my reserves of good memories to push forward through the stifling onset of another eight-month summer.

When Shakespeare wrote in one of his sonnets that "summer's lease hath all too short a date," he was referring, of course, to English summers, not south Florida ones. Certainly for us, summer's lease has a date that's all too long. For one thing, we must listen to eight months of media admonitions about the dangers of hurricanes. As one who went outside on the morning after Andrew to find my neighbor's house without a second story and my own yard without so much as one tree above ten feet tall, I know we all must take precautions against those summer storms. But I find the constant shrill forebodings coming from TV "Storm Centers" to be galling displays of fear-mongering that are clearly meant to raise ratings more than consciousness. The prospect of spending the next eight months closely watching the tropics has become almost as insufferable as the heat.

And then there is the worst part of summer in south Florida. How utterly tormenting it is to sit and watch on TV as the Michigan Wolverines march down the field against Ohio State with one hundred thousand fans cheering from the stadium, bundled in their October sweaters. It simply isn't fair that we have to forgo autumn. Yes, yes, it helps our precious Dolphins because they're prepared to play in the subtropical heat while those wusses from Buffalo have to bring their arctic fans along simply to keep their team upright and breathing. Yes, it's fun to watch the opposing teams wilt in our brutal October heat. But that's small compensation for missing an entire season of the year. And such a glorious one at that.

But when I'm feeling down about the ceaseless

summer heat, I remember what that gentleman in west Broward told the TV reporter several years back when a bale of marijuana tossed from a passing plane exploded through the ceiling of his mobile home and landed at his feet in his living room. "Well," he said, "I guess it's just one of those things you have to put up with to live in paradise."

SPRING RITES

Here it is, spring again, the season to be reborn. Now let's see. Who do I want to be this year?

I usually give myself about a month to decide. Happens every year at this time. At least it has been happening for the last ten years. I finish a novel, ship it off, then I have one month to figure out what I want to obsess over for the next eleven. One month to choose the men and women I'm going to talk to and hang out with most of my waking hours for most of the waking months till this time next spring.

Way back thirty-odd years ago, when I decided to take a grab at this brass ring, I had the impression, after reading Carlos Baker's biography of Ernest Hemingway, that being a writer might be fun. My Hemingway-inspired vision of a typical day went something like this: Wake early, take two aspirin, write till noon. Count the number of words. Five hundred. Good job. Have lunch. Have a couple of beers for lunch. Take a siesta. Wake up midafter-noon, go down to the harbor, crank up the boat, ice down the beer, go out and fish the Gulf Stream. Come in at sunset. Walk down to the local pub. Buy a daiquiri. Buy another one. Talk to men. Talk to women. Talk to more women. Buy another daiquiri and another one. At midnight stumble home, sleep it off. Get up early, two more aspirin, then read the previous day's work, delete half of it. Start writing again. When the novel is done, take a year off to safari in Africa or cover a righteous war for *Look Magazine*. Then, after getting good and ready, stuffed to the brim with incredible new material, sit down and start hammering out those five hundred words a day again. More daiquiris. More aspirin.

Sounded like bliss. Sounded like paradise.

Unfortunately, it's nothing like how it worked out.

My days more closely resemble John D. Mac-Donald's days. I never met the great man, the creator of Travis McGee, but I was lucky enough to speak with his wife shortly before she died. She described his days as being almost completely consumed with work. He got up early and went right to his office. He broke for lunch, but their arrangement was that she would not talk to him during that half hour together so as not to distract him from his considerations of plot and character or alter the mood that he had worked so hard all morning to establish. Then he worked all afternoon. After he ate dinner with the family, the agreement was that John D. would spend the nighttime hours interacting with wife and kids, and he valiantly attempted to comply. But inevitably, his widow told me, John D. would begin pacing around the living room, making increasingly larger circles until finally he got close to the door of his study. Then, without a word, he'd duck away and work till long after everyone was asleep.

John D. MacDonald managed to write two, three, sometimes four novels in one year. It's an astonishing output, especially considering the high quality of his books. Working eight to ten hours a day, usually six days a week, for most of the year, I have been able to eke out only a single book a year. I can't imagine the whirlwind he was riding.

Consequently, a John D. year sometimes had two springtimes, or three, or even four. Multiple seasons when the trees blossomed again, the birds erupted into song, and great buds of optimism flowered in the heart.

One spring a year is about all I can stand.

The yearly cycle looks like this: When the latest book has been carried to term and is finally born, the emptiness of postpartum begins to well in my chest. So I switch off the computer, get up from my chair, go to the door, take an experimental sniff of the air outside, take a slightly deeper, fortifying breath, then step across the threshold and set off.

For the next month I pretend to be a journalist. I interview people. I read books and articles about my chosen subject. I research, take notes. I go places I've never been and observe those places carefully. I ask lots of stupid questions. I educate myself. Before the month is over I have become a quick study know-it-all on my chosen subject matter. In the past I've researched south Florida archaeology, international animal smuggling, fish farming, garbage recycling, pain management research. Each time the subject seemed like the most fascinating, exotic, and earthshaking subject ever written about. Spring is about hope. Spring is about great expectations. Spring is a giddy, silly, forgetful time. A time to lie down in the clover and drowse as if the long, dreary winter never existed.

Then comes summer. Long and hot and luxuriously fertile. Act One, when the characters walk onto the stage and speak their first lines. Everything is so fresh, so full of sap. I'm still drunk with the elixirs of spring, tipsy with all the new knowledge I've acquired. Gushing forth in great spurts of activity, page after page after page.

Fall is another matter altogether. Act Two. The long middle of the book. I know the characters now. I see their flaws, their superficialities. I've explored my subject, seen how complicated it really is, how beyond my reach. I promise myself to choose a more modest topic next time. By autumn's end I've usually gotten my characters into trouble so severe, I'm not sure I can extricate them. I have no idea what my destination is, or how I'm going to get there. There are days when I write for eight hours and all that I can manage is to delete ten pages.

I usually break for Christmas. A day or two to mark the passage of fall becoming winter. I'm grumpy now. This is the time the book always goes badly. By now I dislike my characters, dislike the sound of my own voice, dislike the whole story. I decide to get into another line of work, something I can leave behind at the office. Some occupation in which my entire year's work doesn't wind up in print for anyone to see and criticize. Fishing guide sounds nice.

Now it is dead winter. Act Three. Time to solve the last problems, tie up all the loose ends. But there are so many loose ends I can't possibly do it. I'm irritable and self-involved. I whine a lot. I'm insufferable. I can talk about nothing else but the book I'm finishing. I am author, hear me bore.

The trick of writing the last act is to sit down an hour before dawn in a puddle of Elmer's Glue and peel it off my seat at midnight. Writing becomes an athletic event as much as a literary one. How to keep the back from cramping, how to keep the eyes unblurred.

This is the time my editor usually calls. "So how's the book coming?" The mildest and fairest of inquiries. But it sends me into a final frenzy. I tie up ten thousand loose ends in a day. I tie up more loose ends and more. I have the good guy face his ultimate fear. I see what he is made of. I see what I am made of.

Then one afternoon I walk into the house and announce, "It's done. It's finished."

"So now you can have a life again?" she asks.

I look at her. I think about it.

"Well, maybe I can take the weekend off. We can go stalk some rhino. Or maybe I could cover some righteous war. Drink some daiquiris."

She gives me that acid look.

Ah, spring.

HEMINGWAY

Somehow I made it through high school and college without reading much of Hemingway. Oh, I read a couple of stories. "Hills Like White Elephants" and "The Short Happy Life of Francis Macomber." But I wasn't much impressed. I was a poet back then, and my tastes in fiction ran more toward the lush prose of Durrell or Fowles or John Hawkes. Hemingway's writing seemed anorexic and shallow. And there was a certain disapproving tone in the way my sixties professors referred to him, a condescension toward what those professors must have considered his boorish, self-dramatizing life.

So I have no idea why I picked up a hardback copy of Carlos Baker's biography of Hemingway shortly after it was published in the late sixties. But almost instantly, as I began to read Baker's tome, I was hooked. Baker, like my professors, didn't approve of Hemingway's boisterous life or his self-indulgence or his grand gestures or his barroom fights or his faithlessness to his four successive wives. But for me, a small-town boy still wrestling with defining himself as a writer, reading about the arc of development of one of the greatest writers of our century was an utter joy and a revelation.

For one thing, I saw for the first time that it was possible to be a writer and still be a fully functioning, testosterone-pumping male. So many of the male writers I'd studied in college—Truman Capote, Tennessee Williams, Mark Twain, even Faulkner—lived gaudy, dramatic lives. But unlike Hemingway, most of the male writers whose lives I was the most familiar with were either openly effeminate or had the slightly prissy air of men who spent too much time in literary soirees and not enough standing knee-deep in trout streams.

I was twenty-one at the time. And with the revolution in gender roles in full swing, Hemingway's macho bravura seemed a wonderful corrective. I was a jock and loved the outdoors, and no writer I'd ever read validated these pastimes the way Hemingway did. I remember as I finished that lengthy biography, I wept. In fact, I wept on and off for several days. His suicide hit me hard. I wept for a man I had never met. A man whose work I had not even read. But I wept because I felt some powerful, only half-understood connection with this man of my grandfather's generation. A man who rose to the heights of the literary world. A man loved by many, hated by many more, and misunderstood by almost all.

After I finished that biography, I set about reading the stories and the novels, discovering almost immediately that Hemingway's work was far more subtle and challenging than I'd imagined. His irony is deft, and like all great ironists, Hemingway is a tricky writer. What he says is not always what he means. Sometimes what he says is so deadpan, so flat and toneless, there is almost no way to be sure if he is being ironic or sincere.

A few years later, I was teaching Hemingway to college students, poring over the vast amount of Hemingway criticism and biographies so I could be sure I was bringing my students the latest, best thinking on the man. I still have a copy of *The Sun Also Rises* that I used in that first class. More than a quarter of a century later, my early marginal notes seem incredibly silly. In fact, that copy of *The Sun Also Rises* is the same one I used on several occasions over the decades. It is now a palimpsest of changed opinions, old marginal notes mocked by later ones, and those later ones crossed out by a newly wised-up version of myself. What those notes tell me is that there is no end to Hemingway's challenge.

These days I see in Hemingway's masculine strut, his passion for bullfighting and marlin fishing and boxing and war, an attitude that is wonderfully complex. He's a male chauvinist who wrote stories mocking male chauvinism. He's a war hero who wrote movingly about cowards. He's a great stylist whose style was so simple it was considered radically experimental in his time and yet now has become almost the standard of clear, precise prose. He's a midwestern boy who fled the straitlaced conventions of his time and place and ran off to the wildest and craziest place on the globe, Paris in the twenties, where he proceeded to live an almost ascetic life. He was a drunk who abhorred drunks. He was the manliest writer of our century but a man who continually fantasized and wrote about changing gender. He was tender and tough. He was reckless in his life and utterly controlled in his prose. He developed a code of behavior and ethics that became the moral guidebook for his generation, yet he could not live up to his own standards.

He is for me the greatest, most complicated writer I know and one of the saddest human beings. He's a challenge to almost every would-be author. It was said of Hemingway that he lived it up in order to write it down. And that's one of his most deadly allures. For there will always be those writers who see in Hemingway's showmanship, in his thrill-seeking, big-game-hunting side, a model of what a writer's life should look like: hard drinking, hard living, carpe diem to the tenth power.

But for me, Hemingway's best self is in the writing. His spare, athletic sentences are like tuning forks, their flawless crystalline notes vibrate with utter clarity, challenging us lesser mortals to tune our own ears to their perfect pitch.

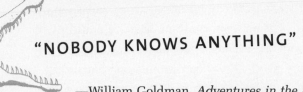

"NOBODY KNOWS ANYTHING"

—William Goldman, *Adventures in the Screen Trade*

ACT 1. PAVLOV

I get a phone call out of the blue, a conference call no less, with three guys telling me how great I am, raving, raving, raving about how much they like my novels, though never actually naming a single title. Which is one of the seven deadly warning signs that you are dealing with film executives.

They go on to say how sorry they are that a recent deal they tried to make with me didn't work out. They wanted to buy all my novels so they could put south Florida on the television map in a series featuring Thorn, the sensitive-wry-macho hero of several of my novels. They don't mention the fact that the deal fell through because they wanted to buy Thorn, lock, stock, and gun barrel, for two dollars and thirty-nine cents.

"How can I help you?" I ask pleasantly.

"Well, since we couldn't steal Thorn from you, we wondered if you'd be stupid enough to agree to come up with a brand-new character as close to Thorn as possible and a whole new story idea so we could steal that from you instead. All you'd have to do is take time away from your normal work and spend a few weeks writing up something that we could pitch to a TV network. All on spec, of course. If what you write is any good, all we can promise is that we'll fly you out here super-economy class to go along to the pitch."

I thought about it for a moment, years of Pavlovian training kicking in—all those fantasies about Hollywood, all those movies consumed, those ten thousand hours of television flickering before my eyes.

"Sure," I said. "I can be that stupid."

And we were off to the LaLa Land races.

ACT 2. *BAYWATCH* WITH PISTOLS

I put my new novel on hold and spend three weeks creating a whole new set of characters, their backgrounds, their relationships, new locations, new dramatic tensions. I sketch out three different stories, potential pilots. The story takes place in the Keys, my fictional stomping ground. It's set at a mom-and-pop motel with a marina. It features a guy named Terry, a thirty-five-year-old with a haunted past who runs the motel, works on the boats, and is called on frequently by his Keys friends to solve their life-threatening difficulties. Creepy, colorful bad guys, witty, off-center dialogue. My trademarks.

I call the Hollywood trio and run the idea by them, and they are ecstatic.

"*Baywatch* with pistols," one of them says.

"*Magnum PI* with a dark Florida edge," says another. "It's hot. Very hot."

"I know it's a lot to ask, after all the work you've put

in," the third one says. "But could Terry be twenty-two instead?"

I gave it a second's weighty consideration.

"Sure," I say. "Why not?"

ACT 3. SALMON SALAD

They fly me to Hollywood. They take me to lunch, buy me a salmon salad, introduce me to a man about my age who is to be the "show-runner." (The guy who runs the show.) He was once a novelist himself but has spent the last ten years writing and producing such shows as *Hill Street Blues* and *Miami Vice* and *NYPD Blues*. He's made millions. Which is millions more than most novelists make.

The show-runner raves about my work. He raves about my TV series idea. He loves the location. Florida is very hot. Florida is where it's happening. Wait till we get down there and start shooting. What fun. Then he proceeds to pick holes in my characters, my situations, my pilots. Brainstorming, it's called. By the end of lunch, Terry is a different guy. Even younger, shallower, hipper, dumber. All in all, more suitable for television.

"So, do you agree?"

The trio looks at me.

"Well, do you?"

"Sure," I say.

"Good. So tomorrow you'll pitch the story idea to the top studio executive."

"Me? Me alone?"

"Don't worry, we'll be there. It's easy. You'll do great."

ACT 4. THE RECEPTION AREA

The next morning in the lobby of the television studio, the show-runner admits he's confused about the pilot story. Why does Terry do this? Why does Terry do that? So we reconstruct the entire story in the reception area. Terry is even shallower now. Just as we finish, we're summoned to the studio executive's office.

ACT 5. TWENTY-THREE YEARS OLD

There are five of us on my team. Together we have published fourteen novels. We have developed and produced and directed successful TV shows and several feature-length movies. Our movies and our television shows and our books are seen and read around the world.

There is one of him.

He's twenty-three. Maybe less. He's in jeans and a T-shirt. He's drinking sparkling water. I'm no ageist. I don't think that if you're older, you're automatically wiser. No sir, I don't think that. But come on, this kid's twenty-three.

I pitch the show. I've never pitched before. I've seen pitches in movies that make fun of Hollywood. Robert Altman's acerbic *The Player,* for instance. I know that this studio executive is going to hear about fifty or so pitches today. But beyond that, all I know about pitches comes from Little League.

The kid is drinking water all through my pitch. He's guzzling the stuff. He's thirsty as hell. Apparently made even thirstier by my description of Terry and his friends and the marina and the colorful bad guys and the new pilot idea that we just created. I finish. He smiles.

"Good," he says. "*Baywatch* with pistols. A blue-skies show. We're looking for that."

We leave.

"Fine, fine," the trio says. "Only next time do it quicker. Cut it in half, two minutes, three. These guys don't have a big attention span."

ACT 6. GREAT JOB

I'm back in Florida. They're right, Florida is hot. Very hot. I get the call. This time it's just one guy on the phone.

"They didn't bite."

"Oh," I say. "They give any reason?"

"It's the Florida thing."

"The Florida thing?"

"They're doing crime and grime this season."

"Crime and grime?"

"You know, gritty urban. Cops with a human side."

"What happened to blue skies?"

"Florida's out."

"Okay, okay, how about Terry runs a mom-and-pop motel and marina in Chicago? Or hey, I've got it. Put Terry on the Hudson River. New York City. There you go."

"Maybe next year," he says. "But you did good. It was a good pitch. A little long, but good."

"Thanks," I say. "Thanks."

Goldman's right. Nobody knows anything. I know less all the time.

AFTER-DINNER CONVERSATION

Not long ago on a perfect south Florida evening, moonlit and mosquito free, while I was sitting out on a friend's patio sharing some after-dinner wine with several intelligent, calm, reasonable people of roughly my own baby boomer age, an argument erupted that was so fierce and rancorous we almost came to blows and I thought for a moment the wineglasses might explode.

We were talking about the war in Vietnam.

Even as I write these words, I can feel my blood pressure begin to rise. And across the fibers of space and time I can feel your own pressure rising as well, dear reader. This is a subject still so densely strewn with emotional land mines that I wonder at my own idiocy for taking it on. But I suppose that alone is reason enough. That we still care so much about that long-ago war, about our own choices then, about the choices of others, that we can still find ourselves ranting and being ranted at after all these years, makes the subject sufficiently remarkable to require at least a short examination.

When I was growing up, my father was still fresh from World War II. I remember almost word for word the few war stories he told. I vividly recall handling his medals and ribbons and his confiscated Luger and an old green ammunition box full of medals he had been obliged to take from German prisoners of war so they couldn't use the pins as weapons. I was always filled with a mix of awe and dread when I handled those icons of war.

Like many boys my age, I watched war movies with a sort of religious ardor. I dreamed of my own war, my own chance to be heroic, to throw myself on a grenade to save my buddies, to carry wounded comrades back to safety, to sneak behind enemy lines and blow up the crucial bridge or ammo dump. I played for hours with army men, staging elaborate battles in my sandpile. I formed the neighbor kids into regiments, and we played war games in the woods around our house. I fantasized about West Point, Annapolis, a life of spit and polish and high command.

In high school, as the dream hardened into more realistic terms, I worked toward gaining an appointment to West Point or the Air Force Academy. I kept my grades up, I worked hard at sports, and most important, I dedicated the largest part of my non-sexual fantasizing hours to reveries about military exploits. It became my intention, if I was not accepted at one of the service academies, to follow in my father's footsteps and my uncle's and my cousin's and attend that now infamous private military college, The Citadel.

In short, a military life was in my blood. It was saturating my marrow. I was a soldier in training throughout most of my youth. I read war stories. I read tomes about World War I and II. I immersed myself in the legends of MacArthur and Eisenhower and Rommel. I even inveigled my parents into sending me to military school for my senior year in high school.

That was 1964, and Vietnam was only the dullest of drumbeats on the distant horizon. But that summer before I left for military school, early in August, exactly thirty-five years ago this week, the USS *Maddox*, a Navy destroyer on a reconnaissance mission in the Gulf of Tonkin, came under fire by three North Vietnamese torpedo boats. The Vietnamese were retaliating, they claimed, for the shelling of several offshore Vietnamese islands by the *Maddox* and its sister ships. More retaliatory strikes followed. And in a matter of days, on August 7, 1964, Congress passed the Gulf of Tonkin Resolution, which gave President Lyndon Johnson authority to take military action against the North Vietnamese. It was this flimsy resolution, not an official declaration of war, that Johnson trotted out for the next four years to justify his continuing escalation of the hostilities.

I'd gotten my war, but it was a lousy one. No solidarity of purpose, no clear-cut outrage. Instead we were given the domino theory. If Vietnam fell, all of Southeast Asia would fall under Communist control, then little by little the rest of the free world would come tumbling down as well. The domino theory was a hard sell. Even gung-ho wannabes like me couldn't quite grasp it. Compared to Pearl Harbor, compared to goose-stepping German troops marching into Paris, it just didn't stir the soul. It was hard to see how such an obscure country on the other side of the globe in any way threatened our freedom. I wanted to believe, I truly wanted to.

Yet by the time I faced my last year of college deferment, I had come to believe that war was a moral issue. Wars were not political or patriotic except in the most superficial sense. What stirred my generation to a frenzy, and stirs us still when we debate again these old issues, is that very fact, that wars are moral acts taken by individuals as well as nations.

And like other major moral quandaries of our time, such as abortion and capital punishment, the war in Vietnam arouses passionate, sometimes violent debate. Good people, reasonable people bitterly disagree. On that evening in our patio debate, one of the two Vietnam vets seemed to go out of his way to provoke the argument by rhapsodizing about his war experience. He said something to the effect that Vietnam was ennobling, an experience of pure joy as the ground shook beneath his feet with mortar fire. He mouthed the platitudes that some politicians at the time were fond of using. Serving our country was an honor. Stopping Communism was a necessary and heroic enterprise. His fellow vet was not as rapturous, but in his quiet way he reinforced his friend's positions. It was the second vet's belief that a young man of eighteen or nineteen should not challenge the authority of his government or question his own responsibility to serve his nation. My country, right or wrong. He went on to say that war protesters and the likes of Jane Fonda had undermined the will of many of his fellow soldiers. And like his fellow vet, he repeated the familiar refrain that upon returning home from the war, they were treated with contempt and revulsion like no other vets in American history.

On the other side that night was a fairly wide range of antiwar sentiment. One of us had actively worked against the war, counseling draft resisters and engaging in legal acts of civil disobedience. He was vehemently opposed to the first vet's glorification of the war. He'd lost friends there and thought our leaders had acted with criminal disregard. And I argued my case—that I deeply wanted to be a soldier, that I had always dreamed of fighting for some righteous cause, but I simply could not accept the morality of this war. And finally, after years of soul-searching and study and reading about the war, I had decided I would have to face jail or permanent exile if I was not allowed a legal exemption from service. My application for conscientious objector status was denied. My appeals were denied. I had taken my physical and passed it despite legitimate letters from doctors testifying to a congenital spinal deformity and a history of disabling back spasms. I was in the process of deciding what part of the country I would go to in order to turn myself in to the authorities, refusing the draft and serving my time in prison, when I received a response to my medical appeal, a deferment letter from the office of the Surgeon General.

For all those good people gathered on that perfect south Florida evening, the Vietnam War was clearly a defining moment. It was probably the most important moral decision any of us ever made or will ever have to make. And like many decisions we made at eighteen, some of us might regret those choices, wish to have made them differently. But clearly all of us who were embroiled in that after-dinner quarrel are still deeply fervent about the moral issues raised by that long-ago war. In some measure, who we became later in life was deeply shaped by the decisions we made about that war. It's hard to imagine that we will ever be finished with it. That we will learn to accept the views of those who chose to do the opposite of what we did. It is hard to imagine that we can forgive or be forgiven by those with whom we so strongly disagree. Though surely we should try. Surely such bottled rage is not good for any of us. Thirty-five years later and with the mere mention of the topic, the hands begin to quiver and the blood pressure soars.

GUNS

Some of my earliest and happiest memories have to do with guns. When I was about ten my father used to take my older brother and me on pleasant autumn tramps through the woods with an old .22 rifle. We tossed beer cans in the river and tried to sink them. We set them on fence posts and tried to send them flying. I remember the lessons he taught me about gun safety, how there was an invisible laser beam that projected from the barrel, and that invisible beam must never come close to a human body. I learned how to carry a rifle and how to load it, how to clean it after shooting.

On those hikes my father tried to instill in me a respect for guns, even a healthy fear of them. From his years in the war, he'd seen what guns could do, and though he rarely shared his war stories, the gravity with which he handled guns conveyed very clear messages about both the horror and the heroism my father associated with firearms.

He kept a German Luger hidden away in an artillery canister high up in his workroom. Once or twice he took it down and allowed me to hold it and revel in its superb workmanship. I remember its heft, its oily odor, its sleekness, its powerful allure. As part of his military duties, he'd confiscated the pistol from a German prisoner of war during the postwar occupation. Somehow he'd smuggled it back to our small midwestern town, and there it stayed, high on a shelf, always unloaded and out of sight, a dreadful reminder of all he'd seen and all he wanted to shield us from.

A year ago I bought a shotgun because I'd developed an interest in sporting clays, a relatively new sport that is a first cousin to skeet shooting. The object is to smash as many of the little orange disks as possible while shooting from a dozen or so different shooting stations that are positioned in a wooded setting. The disks come flying overhead or from right to left or left to right, in swooping arcs or sometimes in skittering bounces across the ground. It's damnably hard and damnably frustrating and a great deal of fun. Out of a hundred clays, the best I've done is fifty-something, but it's really not the shooting that's the attraction. Walking around in the woods with four or five other shooters, all of us trying with varying degrees of futility to keep the barrel moving through the target, trying to squeeze off the shell with a minimum of flinching, all that fine-tuned muscle control that seems just beyond my reach, is exhilarating and often hilarious. And of course, every time I go shooting, I feel faint echoes of those long-ago walks in the woods with my father.

In my novels, I depict violence in many forms. Though I certainly don't intend to glorify violence or the use of weapons as an appropriate way to resolve differences, I write in a genre that tackles issues of crime and evil and brutality, so I've found it necessary to create numerous scenes in which handguns are fired and people are killed. These scenes always make me intensely uncomfortable, both artistically and morally, for they almost always seem too pat, too predictable, genre clichés. But worse than that, I worry that such scenes can be both numb and numbing.

The people who can find no other way to resolve their difficulties than to use a weapon have in some sense gone numb. The boy who kills his teacher, the student who targets other students, the man who opens fire in a church, the man who walks into a daycare center and begins shooting at whatever moves, all these people have lost either temporarily or permanently that empathetic reflex that keeps us human. They don't feel for other people, don't care about other people, but simply follow the black noise screaming in their heads.

And when I create such scenes in fiction, no matter what artistic heights I manage to achieve, I fear I have added to the numbing cascade of similar images that bullet by bullet, scene by murderous scene deaden our hearts, mitigate our outrage, and in some small way harden us to the suffering of others.

When my father took me target shooting in the woods and later allowed me to touch that German Luger, he was careful to convey the serious responsibility involved in handling firearms. It was the same seriousness that he employed when teaching me to drive an automobile. The moment was weighted with the importance of a rite of passage, a major threshold crossed.

If it were only so simple to remedy gun violence by providing improved gun safety training or by enforcing or enacting more gun laws. But of course it isn't that easy. For the lessons our fathers taught us about gun safety were not what made that world a safer and saner place. Those instructions were the smallest part of my overall social education. What my father knew about guns, their dangers and their fit uses, was integral to his larger worldview of civility and respect. There was no moral ambiguity in his view of guns, and there were no situational ethics in his dealings with his fellowman. You didn't point a gun at another human being, ever. It was as simple and straightforward as that. Guns were dangerous, but a part of life. You needed to know how to use them with the greatest care and respect.

While indulging in nostalgia for a kinder, simpler time is no remedy for our current woes, surely there is something we can learn by recollecting our parents' wisdom. When I think of the most important lessons my father taught me about guns, I recall two specific moments: that swift, stern grip he took on my rifle barrel, steering it out of harm's way, and the look of delight in his eyes when I finally sent that beer can flying.

TOUCHY-FEELY

Touchy, touchy, we say to that hypersensitive fellow who takes offense easily. Thin-skinned or calloused is the way we describe the emotional range of our fellowman. Skin is everywhere in our language and for good reason. It is the largest organ by far, both in volume and in mass (an organ being a group of cells performing a similar function). We can close our eyes, plug our nose or ears, we can shut our mouths to sweet and sour, but we cannot stop feeling the touch of the world. It is with us even in our dreams as our back slides along silk sheets or cotton, flannel, or synthetic. We are registering impressions every second, pressures and heat, the slickness of glass, the burr of a nail file. We are bombarded by the prickly world, its bristles and stubble, its razor-sharp edges, its flakiness and nubs and scuffs and bruises, its breezes and the weight of sunlight on our shoulder, the tacky goo of spilled Coke on the car seat, the feathery down of a cat's tail, the whiskery softness of a loving caress.

And that's just the skin our clothes don't hide.

Intimacy is touch's middle name. The density of nerve endings in those private places that engorge with blood and flood the brain with happy chemicals have no equal in the other senses. Yes, we love the smell of our lover. Yes, we love to see her shape and swaying walk. We love the pitch of her voice and the taste of her breath. But skin is the way we love her, skin is the way we send our most private messages. Smoothing our hands across her flesh, tweaking and dabbing, massaging her neck, scratching our fingernails into her scalp, tickling the places only we have discovered. Our own hands working on our own skin never have the same success. A muted pleasure at best. What moves us is contact with the foreign world, my skin against her skin, tugging the delicate hairs where the densest sense receptors lie, or probing those hidden folds, those moist and secret places that with the right stroke, the right pressure and cadence will push us beyond reason, make our hearts soar, our pulses quiver, our juices flow.

The coils of the ear, the tiny webs between our fingers, the soft pocket above our clavicle, the armpit, the back of the knee. We can put our minds in our skin, feel ourselves from inside out. The sutured pucker of our navel, tender and secret. The ruff of down on the cheek. The ticklish arch of the foot. Every inch of skin has its identity. A voice, a distinct tingle. The *hara,* a place below the navel that some believe is the body's center of gravity. I've been there, put my mind there, felt deeply anchored to the earth, not so top-heavy as when my mind is in my skull. It is touch from the inside out.

We even receive the world through our feet. Sand in our shoes, a sandbur snagged in our socks, a blister, a corn, a thickened callus. We can distinguish the powdery sands of Saint Augustine from the hard-packed beach at Daytona by taking one barefoot step. We have felt the dull slice of a broken beer bottle hidden in the sand. There is a glop of warm tar inside the slime of seaweed. It coats our foot and must be scrubbed away with astringent alcohol. We feel the hundred harmless broken seashells bristling against our soles, and as we wade into the sea, there is the brush of some frightened sea creature trying to stay out of our way. And then there's the sea itself. Its welcoming buoyancy, lifting us, cooling us, relaxing the pores; floating on it, submerging in it, the silky slide against our skin. We are water ourselves and salty at that, given to tidal pressures from the moon. We swim in the amniotic fluids of our earth, as we swam so long ago like blind fish in the womb. Our first sensation was that watery place, the touch of our mother's inner tissues against our own.

Then, of course, there is the sunburn. The skin, they tell us now, never forgets. It is a parchment on which is written every glorious afternoon floating on the pool, every moment with the top down, every ticktock of radiation that the sun sent our way. It's all there, still glowing in some substrata of the skin's memory. We learn that sunburned skin is so sensitive to the touch because of its relative abundance of prostaglandins. Which is why NSAIDs (nonsteroidal anti-inflammatory drugs like Advil and aspirin) work so well to reduce the pain of sunburn, especially when taken *before* exposure to the sun. But who among us would subtract from our history that glorious sunny day when we stood shirtless on the deck of a boat all morning and caught our limit of dolphin, or that crystalline afternoon when we fell asleep on the beach in Key West, a drink at our side, a good book in our lap. Yes, my skin remembers every insult, every extra prickle of the sun's rays. But I'll gladly offer my arms and shoulders up to the scalpel if I can enjoy the occasional sun saturation that produces that glow, the flush and smolder in the subcutaneous zones, a feeling of fullness and harmony with the natural world that is so heady it probably should be illegal.

And the tongue. Ah, the tongue with its wet, delicious, sluglike presence. Which can feel the popcorn kernel between the teeth, the rind, the nagging ragged edge of a new filling, or reach out through the tender lips and touch the world, smear its length across a postage stamp or the sticky edge of an envelope, or sense the thickness of a malted shake or touch the fiery tip of another's tongue, duel with it, probe and flick. If taste is limited to only four senses, those four are multiplied by a thousand textures and densities, the rich, slick glossiness of crème brûlée, the graininess of grits. We eat oysters because they feel good going down, and those that hate them hate that mucous touch, the slimy feel. The crunch of a good conch fritter, the crispy flake of a perfect crust. It's the tongue's magic, the muscular red worm that lives in our mouth and loves to taste certain words. The bump and grind of nursery rhymes is as much an attraction of touch as sound. The tongue twister, the multisyllabic aerobic workout of a foreign tongue. We wag our tongues and love to talk and love to feel the words take shape in the echo chamber, the orchestra pit of our mouth.

Florida loves to touch. We love to walk seminaked from jungle heat to frigid mall, to watch the chills rise on our arms. We love the wind before a summer storm rolls in off the Everglades, stirring our hair, the follicles aquiver. We love to slog through the surf, to feel the undertow pulling the earth from under our bare feet. We touch the razor edge of sawgrass, test its blade. We are barometric pressure sensors, feeling that first approaching cold front change the air. We feel fall through our skin, absorb it, feel the lift in our pulse. The relief of a drop of only two or three degrees. We are subtle sensors. We know seventy percent humidity from ten points lower or higher. We squeeze our avocados and know exactly the tenderness we want. We thump our melons with our finely calibrated knuckles, run our fingertips across the Braille of their hide. We are machines of touch, attuned to ten thousand competing sensations every millisecond. We sort them out, choose among them, decide what we will feel, what will touch us. Our mosquitoes land feathery soft on the flesh and try so hard not to be noticed, their flimsy legs touching down; then they bend to their work, setting their hair-thin needles, delicately stinging. We slap ourselves, we slap our necks, our ankles, the backs of our opposite hands. We slap ourselves silly.

And then, of course, there is pain. Ecstasy gone awry. Though the opposite of pleasure may not be pain at all, but numbness. The man suspended in a sensory deprivation tank, feeling nothing for hours at a time, will go mad, hallucinate at least, his brain trying every trick to keep the body feeling. Pain is the rough under-edge of pleasure. Without one, we can't know the other. We mingle the two in our greatest moments. Sex, athletics, the performing arts. Endorphins kick in and flood the body with natural morphine to neutral-ize the terrible pain of the marathoner. Mild pain brightens the nerves, gives us that flush, that rush, that sense of overcoming.

Much is being done these days to alleviate pain. My baby boomer generation has a different attitude toward pain than our parents had. The stiff upper lip and uncomplaining, pain-suppressing attitudes have given way to whining and hypersensitivity. We are reaching for the Advil at every twitch. We want our pharmaceuticals, aren't afraid of them as our parents were. We have indulged in recreational drugs and know their powers. So we are consumers of bottled relief. We have sent the signals to the medical world, and they are scrambling to answer our call.

Pain management is now a specialty. Anesthesiolo-gists have made a fast migration from laughing gas to electronic implants in the spine that disrupt the flow of pain messages with bursts of white noise. There are morphine pumps worn beneath the skin, dosing at reg-ular intervals through the day. There are trigger-point injections and acupuncture and twilight drugs, which keep us awake through painful procedures, then wash our memories of the unpleasantness afterward.

Pain is subjective. Pain in England is not the same as pain in Italy. Our thresholds are culturally set, our expectations, our willingness to endure hurt. A pain doctor must sort through one patient's resistance to admitting pain and separate it from another patient's intense receptiveness. People lie about their pain. They don't admit it to themselves or others, or they cringe at every bump, complain, complain, complain. Some people suffer from chronic pain in which, after prolonged torment, the neural pathways in the brain have been rewired so that even when the underlying medical cause of the pain has been remedied, the patient continues to experience the pain. The brain doesn't catch up to the new condition. The script has been rewritten, but the brain continues to receive messages that the body is no longer sending.

And there are extreme cases in which normal touch becomes excruciating. The usual neural pathways of touch, typically using the A-delta nerve fibers in the skin, begin sending pain messages instead. These afferent messages travel to the spinal cord and brain and are interpreted as pain rather than touch. Cutting the usual pain pathways in the spinal cord, called the spinothalamic tract, only works for patients in chronic pain for months. After that the A-delta fibers adapt, and pain is felt via new pathways.

Allodynia is the feeling of pain when the skin is touched or stroked in a nonpainful manner. The patient with allodynia describes the sensation as burning or searing or stinging, and the level of hypersensitivity can be so severe that it's triggered by nothing more provocative than a summer breeze. Silk sheets are a torment, a kiss is agony.

We can trick ourselves out of pain. Placebos work a third of the time. Simply by believing in relief we can experience relief. Self-hypnosis, prayer, meditation, the disciplined reorganization of the brain process.

Some doctors believe that is exactly what is at work in touch therapy, a mind-over-matter, wishful-thinking process that claims to cure us of various ills by a simple laying on of hands. Massage, sustained touch. There are centers now that devote themselves to skin-to-skin treatments of various kinds. Premature babies laid belly to belly with their parents show accelerated development. Is it real? Is it bogus? The evidence is persuasive. And surely we must trust in the power of touch to transform. The power of touch to open us beyond ourselves, to admit the presence of another into our isolated bag of skin.

We wear our soft parts on the outside. The skin is not a shell or exoskeleton, it is an organ with more receptors than any other. We touch and are touched every second of every day. We bathe in stimuli. Are bombarded by a constant meteor shower of taps and pats and slaps and punches and heat and cold and tickles and kisses and hugs and hand-holding and feet rubbing and the infinite surfaces of the world. From the moment we first come squalling into the light, we are touched and touching. It is what we do all day. We feel our way forward. We touch the world, and it touches back. And even in the blackest hours of the night, blind, walking through a soundless house, smelling nothing, tasting nothing, we feel the rug beneath our feet, feel the air flowing across our skin, touch the slick high-gloss surface of the wall, and we know we are alive.

FRESH STARTS

The sun was streaming through the windows that Thanksgiving afternoon. At the head of the table, my grandfather set his fork down on his empty plate, patted his lips with his napkin. His bald head was gleaming. Sharp November light glinted off the silver gravy bowl and the platter where the remains of the turkey and dressing lay. I remember it all with utter clarity even though it happened over forty years ago. We were just finishing the meal when Granddaddy asked the question that froze that moment in my mind for all time. Surely his intent was only to test the budding math skills of his grandson, but his innocent query forever changed the way I considered my life.

"So, Jimmy, can you tell us, How old will you be in the year two thousand?"

I don't recall how long it took to do the math. I was eight years old at the time but was pretty good with addition and subtraction. When I came up with the right answer, fifty-two, my grandfather nodded approvingly.

"Almost as old as I am right now."

"And seventeen years older than I am," my father said.

"So how old will you be in two thousand?" I asked my grandfather.

"Oh, by then I'll be long gone."

He was right. And my father didn't live to see the century roll over either. Although I mourn their loss greatly, it is not them I think of when I recall that Thanksgiving dinner. What I remember is how the years suddenly stretched out before me into the stunning, unknowable distance. The end of the century, forty-four years away, a dizzying, unfathomable span of time. For a child of eight who had never looked farther down the road than to the next holiday or summer vacation, that moment packed a profound existential wallop.

The idea that I would ever be my grandfather's age, or older than my father at that moment, was unthinkable. I puzzled on this remarkable concept for hours on end. It was to be my first intellectual watershed, the moment when I began to wrestle with one of the great mysteries of the human condition: our relationship to time.

Like all the other watershed moments in my life, this one came unexpectedly, a life-changing ambush. Like that phone call I received one morning ten years ago from a virtual stranger in New York notifying me that my first novel had been accepted. It was a moment that would forever alter the nature of my work life and even my sense of self, yet it came sailing out of the blue as unpredictably as a red hot meteorite. No warning, no way to prepare for the long, life-changing set of consequences. Or the afternoon when I received in the mail a Florida lottery ticket filled in with a young woman's phone number. "This could be your lucky day," she said. And boy, was she right. A year later I married her, and for the last decade I've been a different person than I was before that lottery ticket arrived. Never happier, never more thankful.

Or that afternoon at happy hour when the phone rang, and I set my wineglass down and picked up the receiver. And without preamble, my father said, "I'm afraid I've got bad news." And another sea change was under way; the long unraveling of his health had begun, as well as a profound restructuring of my family dynamics and my own sense of mortality.

That's how it's always been. Meteor showers.

So even though it's a new century and one that I've been more or less anticipating since I was eight years old, I feel no great swell of excitement as it arrives. For I have found that the tick of the clock is numbingly constant and the calendar blindly goes about its inexorable business with no regard for our expectations or hopes. In fact, it seems to me that the cycle of anticipation and deflation that many of us experience around the holidays is a measure of how deeply we long for a tidiness that our universe simply doesn't provide. On some subconscious level we seem to yearn for a synchronicity between historical watershed moments and personal ones. Even though that rarely occurs, we still hope. Wouldn't it be nice, wouldn't it be wonderfully harmonious if on New Year's morning we took a deep breath, dusted ourselves off, and suddenly began marching to that different drumbeat we always wanted to attempt? But it doesn't work that way.

Sure, we strain mightily to make ourselves over. And sometimes we're marginally successful. Through discipline and hard work we re-create a sleeker version of ourselves, or a smarter, updated model. We jog and diet, nip and tuck our faces and our psyches. We limber our bodies with yoga and change our diets to whole grains. We quit smoking, join a book club, go on a cruise, donate our time to some worthwhile charity. But those are little nudges to our behavior or our appearance or our sense of self, relatively superficial adjustments to who we are, not the character-defining transformations I'm talking about.

More than likely this next hundred-year stretch is going to give us even more opportunities to revolutionize our bodies, our minds, our careers, and the way we spend our leisure time. We will no doubt have abundant chances to rewrite the script of our lives in ways we cannot at this moment imagine. But then I'm reminded of a question I frequently pose to my fiction writing students. It's one of the fundamental tenets of good writing that a fictional character must change during the course of a story, or there is really no story at all. So I ask them, Do people change? Do they truly change? And usually in the ensuing argument, the class divides along familiar lines.

No one changes, some of them argue. Every person establishes their basic character at an early age; part of that character is inherited, the rest of it is the result of early imprinting, and once our personality is set, each of us coasts along through our next seven or eight decades more or less on psychological autopilot. Oh, sure, we may give up cigarettes or get divorced, but basically we follow preordained patterns. We're mainly happy or mainly sad, we're irritable or celebratory, fairly smart or fairly dumb, and we can only modify those predispositions ever so slightly.

And the other side, the optimists, point to all our major institutions: hospitals heal people, universities educate them, churches save them. Is that not change? Isn't grace or a college education fundamental transformation? When a man is cured from cancer and has faced death and won a temporary reprieve, isn't he different? Isn't he fundamentally changed? And what about love? Doesn't love change our very cell chemistry?

Well, I don't know if we can truly change or if we only fool ourselves into believing we do. This is one of a number of Very Important Questions I'm still working on. In some sense I'm still that eight-year-old boy staring at the silver platter glittering with November light. Full of perplexed wonder at the infinity of seconds and minutes and hours that stretch away before me—all those endless years that must come and go before that boy reaches the millennium. That eight-year-old boy has not changed a bit. Still doing the math in his head. Still locked in that amazing moment, just beginning to ponder something he still hasn't figured out and may never.

CAR WARS

My wife was in a car accident this week. A minor fender bender. Nothing to get excited about. A guy made a left turn in front of her. She had the green light and the right of way, and he was in the opposing right turn lane and just decided, what the hey, he'd turn left. Although the driver lied about what happened, the position of the two vehicles told the tale, and he got the ticket.

Surprise, surprise, he had no insurance, an invalid license, and something was fishy about his registration. I asked the Florida Highway Patrol officer how common that was, no insurance. "Oh, these days it's gotten a lot better. Maybe only thirty to forty percent don't have insurance." Only?

As far as I know this accident wasn't one of the one-third caused by road rage. This guy was simply making an illegal left turn. He didn't seem angry, just dazed and maybe a little confused about driving customs in this country.

But the incident made me consider once again the incredibly stressful and chaotic nature of driving in south Florida, this absolutely necessary and absolutely maddening activity that has become so central to our daily survival.

There was a time in the dim long ago that I actually loved to drive my car. Getting behind the wheel put an extra bounce in my pulse. I considered driving to be somewhere between a sport and a religious art form. I used to seek out twisty back lanes that tested my car's agility and my own reflexes. I felt about my car as cowboys must feel about their horses. To be a good driver was, among other things, to become one with your vehicle.

Of course, in south Florida these days, becoming one with your car takes on a far more ghoulish meaning. And now when I feel that intense pounding in my pulse I realize it's probably some version of road rage. Or maybe it's just terror.

My current disenchantment with driving all began for me one morning back in the eighties when I was headed south on the Palmetto Expressway and a fellow traveler in a silver BMW cut me off. I was whizzing along at sixty or so, and this guy flew by me in the adjacent lane, then with heedless abandon cut into the space I'd left between me and the car in front. The beamer missed my bumper by a whisker. For years I'd tried to follow the driver's ed rule of thumb for proper following distance, leaving a car's length for every ten miles an hour of speed. But as anyone who's driven in south Florida can tell you, leaving a proper following distance is an invitation for seven or eight idiots to sneak in front of you and push you farther and farther away from your destination.

Anyway, that morning on the expressway, I flashed my lights at the BMW, and without thinking, I made an obscene gesture, and before I knew it, the silver car was cruising along beside me and the young man stared over at me with a cruel and disdainful look as if to say, "Oh, god, now I'm going to have to discipline another of these people."

He pulled in behind me and proceeded to tailgate me for fifteen miles through dense traffic and off the exit ramp and onto the surface streets of Kendall. For the next twenty minutes he stayed behind me at every turn, running red lights to do it, taking risk after risk to stay on my bumper. I tried to convince myself that it was just a coincidence, we happened to be traveling to roughly the same destination. But before long I couldn't kid myself anymore and was starting to search for a police station to pull into.

Finally, running low on gas and unable to find a police station or shake the guy, I decided to face my fate. I pulled into the parking lot of a bank. The guy pulled up beside me and slid his window down. We were face to face headed in opposite directions, driver side to driver side.

"You shouldn't shoot birds at people in traffic," he said.

"Why's that?" I asked, though I knew full well why such a thing was dangerous.

"Because you could get shot," he said.

Then we spent roughly thirty seconds staring at each other in silence, establishing alpha dog status. It felt like the final moments of *High Noon*. Surely he was armed. Surely he wouldn't have followed me all that way simply to pass on a tidbit of urban wisdom. Surely it must have occurred to him that I might be holding my own Mac-10 just below window level. We were dueling with unseen weapons.

So, I blinked. Fine by me if he wanted to be the alpha dog.

"Thanks," I said, my voice squeaking.

And he gave me the curt, dismissive nod of one who has decided to let an inferior creature go on living.

In the years following that incident I have rarely used my lights or my finger in anger. Though there was one memorable day a few years later when I used my horn again. In my first week of a year's stay in El Paso, Texas, I was sitting in traffic several cars back from the intersection. When the light turned green and the cars did not begin to move in six one-hundredths of a second (or whatever the exact instant is that we south Floridians have determined as the grace period for dawdling drivers), I honked. I wasn't in a hurry. It was simply a south Florida reflex.

I remember vividly the shocked looks on the faces of the nearby drivers as they all swung in my direction. "Is he having a heart attack?" "Does he need our help?" Apparently, no one had ever honked his horn in El Paso, Texas, before.

In time I came to discover that there was little reason to hurry in southwest Texas. No matter where you were headed, there wouldn't be much waiting for you when you get there. And I also learned that El Paso's water supply is contaminated with naturally occurring lithium, which helps to give the citizens that wonderfully drowsy outlook on traffic delays.

Back in south Florida after my year of imbibing Texas water, I cruised the south Florida streets and thoroughfares at the same languid pace I'd come to favor in lithium land. That lasted about a week. And then the lane hoppers, the cell phone gabbers, the false eyelash appliers and beard shavers got to me again.

Sometimes I get nostalgic about that era when red lights still had meaning. Now they seem no more than the merest suggestion that a driver might want to stop unless he is in too much of a hurry. And I fondly recall that distant age when drivers still used turn signals. Nowadays nobody seems to know what that lever's for. Or else they're all eating burgers and chugging Cokes, steering with their knees, and simply don't have a hand free to use the signal. And of course, using a turn signal requires advance thought, while most south Florida drivers don't seem to know what they're about to do until they do it.

I have driven in Paris, London, Mexico City, Italy, Madrid, Berlin, Los Angeles, Boston, Manhattan, and most of the rest of America's largest cities. I have never seen drivers less aware of the rules of the road or less concerned about their fellow travelers anywhere. Perhaps it's partly due to our vaunted cultural diversity—everyone is playing by a different set of driving rules, the rules they learned back home. A great tower of driving babble.

Or maybe it's something darker and more scary than that. The final death throes of courtesy. A me-first nihilism that has as its only rule: If you can get away with it, it's okay.

In such a world there's little we can do except make sure our insurance premiums are paid up and that we have a rental car provision in our policy. It's either that or move to El Paso permanently. And as bad as things are on the highways of south Florida, they're not that bad yet.

DISNEY VIRUS

Lately I've heard with growing frequency the terms
Disney virus and *Disneyfication* used to describe
that peculiar Florida penchant for falsifying or
making adorably cute some part of our natural
landscape. For example, the Disneyfication of Key
West has been proceeding for decades as more and
more concrete monstrosities replace the elegantly
ramshackle native homes. In an attempt to make
these new behemoths blend into their surroundings, the concrete architects add tin roofs or some
inch-deep facade in a futile effort to duplicate the
quaint and authentic structures they've destroyed.

But most of the time the Disney virus doesn't
destroy and replace, it simply fills some beautifully
empty piece of terrain with a new, adorably cute
creation. In suburban development after suburban
development—the Willow Traces, the Hawk's Quays,
the Manatee Moorings—theme park–inspired devel-
opers whip up fantasylands that mean to transport their new inhabitants to dreamy villages of
yesteryear, communities where people are suddenly

relieved of their modern stresses and begin to act in the polite and civil way of those model citizens we know and love so well: Mickey and Minnie.

Actually, the Disney virus was playing havoc with Florida long before Walt bought up central Florida and covered it with colorful plastic. Blame it on Ponce de León and his boys. Call it *Leonification* or the *Ponce De virus*. For Ponce's pursuit of the Fountain of Youth still reverberates powerfully just below the sandy surface of this long peninsula. From its earliest days, Florida's raison d'être has been to satisfy the mythic need to renew oneself, to find a second chance. And throughout our state's history, any number of utopian dreamworlds have taken root here. Merrick's Venetian fantasies became Coral Gables, Opa Locka's creators favored a *Thousand and One Nights* Arabian theme, and on and on. From almost the first, we have gladly permitted our landscape to be reconfigured by any citizen, no matter how daffy he may be, as long as he is in possession of sufficient cash. As a recent ad campaign for the South Florida Chamber of Commerce put it, "Come on down, the rules are different here." Which of course translates to "There aren't any, so feel free to make up your own."

Those of us who worry about the Disneyfication of Florida are concerned that the natural wonders of the state will, one by one, be appropriated by the theme park bandits, and someday soon we will have to stand in line to buy tickets to see The Real Authentic Everglades Re-created in Reynolds Plastic Wrap or Undersea Adventure of the Coral Reef at One-tenth Scale.

In fact, it wouldn't surprise me, in the new totally

Disneyfied Florida, if there were an effort to nudge the state capitol a couple of hundred miles west from its present location to that bastion of nostalgia, that apotheosis of cute and quaint and charming, Seaside, Florida.

For the last decade, on eighty acres of gorgeous Panhandle beachfront land, Seaside has been taking shape under the rigorously watchful gaze of Robert Davis. As the story goes, Mr. Davis and his wife wanted to build a new Florida town on the land they owned, so they spent a great deal of time studying authentic "vernacular" Florida architecture, then handed over their research to a couple of Miami architects so they could modernize the authentic designs of the early Florida cracker builders. The resulting Seaside building code requires such cracker holdovers as tin roofs, wraparound porches, widow's walks, double-hung windows, French doors, and gazebos. The town is laced with sandy footpaths that are bordered by local beach grasses and native vines. No sodding is allowed. All yards are covered with pine mulch. All fences must be wooden pickets, and no two are permitted to be alike.

Pastel paints prevail, peaches and butterfly yellows and pale purples, all of which give the town a rainbowy, Crayola feel. When you approach Seaside from the north along the beach road, making a big sweeping turn, the town springs into view all at once, rising from the barren landscape like some frothy meringue, a colorful clutter of Victorian dollhouses.

Six times I've stayed at Seaside, and on each occasion I've been plagued by acute symptoms of Disney virus exposure. A powerful ambivalence sweeps over me. I find myself grinning idiotically, fondly amused by the capriciousness of the architecture, by the silly names the owners have given their Shangri-la beach houses, by the in-your-face nostalgia-mongering that greets you at every turn. So much wicker, so many Adirondack chairs. Even the rust dappling some of the tin roofs seems planted there. And that's the other side of things. It's all so terribly phony. So contrived, so mannered. The beauty is so manufactured, so orchestrated that I begin to wonder if it is beautiful at all.

This, of course, is the ultimate danger of the Disney virus. We begin to lose our way. The purveyors of the new nostalgia, at Seaside and its many imitators (including Disney's own town, Celebration), are so good at what they do, and we are so hungry to believe that by turning back the architectural clock we can promote a more relaxed and civil existence, that we are all too easily lulled into accepting the fantasy.

I walk along the cobblestone streets, watching the towheaded kids ride their brand-new replicas of ancient bicycles down to the beach, and for a moment I am Norman Rockwell and all is right with the world. Never mind that almost no one actually lives there year-round, Seaside's seductiveness is irresistible. And indeed, compared to the bungee-jumping, go-cart, Goofy Golf Mecca twenty miles away in either direction and the concrete condos that loom just over the horizon, Seaside's scale and use of native flora and vernacular styles seem absolutely enlightened. And it seems deeply uncharitable, downright cynical to object to the artificiality of Seaside. After all, isn't all our "vernacular" architecture stolen from elsewhere?

Maybe so.

But it seems to me that it's one of our jobs as Floridians, a task unique to the citizens of this state, to vaccinate ourselves with a strong dose of skepticism, or else little by little we're apt to trade away our gloriously ramshackle paradise for these safely repackaged versions. And before we know it, we'll be living in a place concocted by cartoonists.

DRY TORTUGAS

Okay, it was a boondoggle. Let's get that out of the way up front. I plead guilty to the flagrant misuse of public funds. Nolo contendere. I admit I have helped fleece America in one of the most egregiously fraudulent enterprises imaginable. The scam even had a code name. Among us elite insiders, we super-grifters, the project was known as the Great Dry Tortugas Novel.

However, I hasten to add that this was an art scam, and as anyone who is familiar with arts budgets anywhere will tell you, most art capers are by their very nature small potatoes. I estimate that I only managed to raise the federal debt by some-where in the neighborhood of a measly three hun-dred dollars, most of which was the round-trip cost for the seaplane that runs between Key West and Fort Jefferson in the Dry Tortugas. The balance of that nonwhopping sum went to pay for my non-extravagant digs at the fort, a two-room apartment that sometimes houses legitimate dignitaries such as Connie Mack and Bruce Babbitt. Why these politicians feel it necessary to visit the southernmost national park, I will leave to your imagination. But surely it has something to do with national defense secrets and the crucial nesting habits of the sea turtle.

My caper started with an innocent enough letter from a park ranger at Fort Jefferson who had decided that it would be appropriate to celebrate National Park Week by having a famous writer visit the island and help in a little project she'd devised. As the joke goes, since she knew no famous writers, she invited me. I found out later that she'd once tried to read one of my novels but had abandoned it because she found it too intense. Nevertheless, for reasons that elude me still, she decided I was exactly the kind of writer her project needed.

The proposal was that I would come to the island and spend all or part of a week some seventy miles away from phones and televisions and interstate gridlock, guiding the creation of a story that was to be dubbed the Great Dry Tortugas Novel. I would write the first paragraph, and any interested visitors to the park would read the previous material and then sit down at a typewriter that the park ranger had set up in a particularly romantic corner of the fort and add their two cents. Additionally, I was to read the mutating work from time to time during my stay and try to nudge it back onto some semblance of a logical course. When the week was up, I would take the story home and add on the final pages, bringing it to the harmonious and satisfying conclusion to which she assumed (but could not bring herself to find out for sure) I brought my own novels.

The whole thing sounded so wacky and impractical that I could do nothing but accept.

So, early in the spring, I tore myself away from my work and drove down to Key West to catch a ride on my own private federally funded seaplane. As we were taxiing out the runway that morning, John, my pilot, noticed that I was staring at his bare feet on the control pedals. He grinned across at me giddily and yelled through the thunderous racket, "It took me twenty years to find a place where I could get paid to fly barefoot." That should have been fair warning.

Though I live in the center of urban south Florida, I've always prided myself on having carved out a tranquil, isolated pattern of existence. Sandals, shorts, and T-shirts, ninety percent of the time. I thought I knew laid-back, but I was about to discover what true tranquillity was all about.

We lifted off and sailed low over the pleasant jumble of Key West, then arced west and south and headed out to sea. The sky was scrupulously clean that day, and below us the water was bluer than blue, with patches of translucent jade and emerald. John coasted low across the sea, and I watched as dozens of sharks and rays plied their ominous trade, and a solitary sailboat leaned into the breeze.

In twenty minutes we were passing over the atoll of the Marquesas Islands, and then farther out we seemed to cross some magical boundary. We were still in the United States, but that was only the sheerest technicality. Those empty waters were wild and growing wilder with every mile. We were a long, long way from the nearest Publix.

I'd seen photographs of Fort Jefferson and had read up on the place in the week prior to my junket. I knew its walls were eight feet thick and fifty feet high and its perimeter roughly half a mile long. Built in 1846, it was considered "The Gibraltar of the West," strategically located to protect shipping lanes from New Orleans to the Straits of Florida. And years later, when it was found to be militarily obsolete, it served as a prison, "America's Devil's Island." Its most famous inmate was Dr. Samuel Mudd, who treated John Wilkes Booth's broken leg and as a result was judged to be part of the conspiracy to kill Lincoln.

I was expecting a tall brick hexagonal structure surrounded by a moat, a humble, slightly eccentric edifice. But as my barefoot pilot tipped the plane into a dramatic bank so I could catch the full panorama of the island all at once, I was utterly enthralled. It is such an extravagant and whimsical design, at once imposing and absurd, as if the architect had been torn between two competing models, fairy-tale castle and grim, practical fortress.

The young park ranger who'd devised the Great Dry Tortugas Novel scheme met the plane and gave me a quick tour of the fort on the way to my spartan apartment. I also had a look at the writing area where the would-be novelists were supposed to be hammering away. The table was arrayed with an electric typewriter, a stack of inky pages, a stiff chair, and a half-empty bottle of gin. Ah, yes, the writer's tools.

Once I'd explored the fort and met the few Sierra Club revelers who were camping on the beach, and after I'd stared up at the hundred frigate birds hovering in the thermals above those heated bricks, I had nearly exhausted the entertainment possibilities of the Dry Tortugas. By my first nightfall I had begun to sink into that timeless, soporific zone where I would wallow for the duration of my visit. For as I was coming to understand, there was nothing to do at Fort Jefferson. Profoundly less than nothing.

Let this be a warning to you, fellow travelers. Go there if you must. Visit one of your national treasures. But there is nothing to do but gaze out at the water, snorkel its limited reef, catch a fish or two from the dock, and watch thousands of sooty and noddy terns fight for nesting space on nearby Bush Key. Nothing, nothing, nothing at all. It is one large hexagonal brick sensory-deprivation tank. And don't forget, those tanks have been known to drive healthy folks insane.

The so-called novel wrote itself with only the barest guidance from me. I was too busy to help in any serious way, busy being swept up by the constant sea breezes moaning through the labyrinthine corridors, the ghostly, mesmerizing haunt of those thick brick walls, which lulled me deeper and deeper into my dream state, an almost hallucinatory somnolence that was a dozen times more restful than its nighttime counterpart.

My single sport was sitting out on my balcony and tossing scraps of food into the moat after dark just so I could hear the large snappers and sharks that lived there surge and splash for the morsels. I wound up throwing them so much of the food I'd lugged along that by the end of my stay the fish began to recognize my silhouette and churned the water even as I rose to my feet.

But mainly I stared out to sea. I stared and stared,

and the sea never changed. But that didn't keep me from staring more.

Four days later, while I waited for the seaplane to take me back to the mainland, a new visitor full of the same hustle and bustle I'd arrived with asked me what I'd been doing on the island for the last few days. And I turned to the young man and smiled in a way that seemed to make him uneasy, and I said with complete sincerity, "Nothing, absolutely nothing."

And yes, I want to confess in this public forum that I am deeply ashamed to have wasted your tax dollars in such a loathsome act of dissipation. I plead guilty in the first degree. In fact, I believe it is only fair I should be severely punished for such gross malfeasance. If I might be so bold as to suggest—how about six months without chance of parole at that dreaded offshore prison site, Fort Jefferson, Dry Tortugas?

THE SMALLEST CHRISTMAS TREE

We usually try to find the largest Christmas tree on the lot. Our ceiling is very high, and it can handle a twelve-footer easily. Although we don't have children, we have always celebrated Christmas as though we did—with lots of lights and angels and snowmen, and on the mantelpiece we assemble one of those corny snow-coated villages with banks and churches and opera houses and people ice-skating on a mirror pond and barber's poles and park benches and a fire truck with its Dalmatian.

However, last year we bought the smallest tree we've ever had, and we opened up only one or two of the many boxes of yuletide decorations we store in the attic. We had to force ourselves to do even that. My wife and I didn't feel much like celebrating because both of us were still recovering from a nasty brush with south Florida crime.

This is a story I never wanted to write. Certainly I have no desire to relive the nightmare of those hours and days, and I've also hesitated because I wasn't certain my writing skills were up to the task.

There are just so many ways the telling of this story can go wrong. Most worrisome is the possibility that in recounting my wife's ordeal and putting my story alongside it, I might suggest that my distress was in any way equal to hers. It was not. It was not even close.

Near the end of June, about five o'clock on a drizzly gray afternoon with the sky hovering at the treetops, an oppressive day with an airless breeze, I was in the kitchen peering into the refrigerator, searching for predinner snack.

At the same time, she was on her way home from her high school teaching job and was making some of her usual stops—grocery, cleaners, mall, bookstore. It was in the parking lot of the bookstore that it happened.

After parking in the closest spot to the entrance she could find, a place at the rear of the building, she hurried through spitting rain into the store. She didn't locate the book she was looking for, so she was only inside for five minutes. She walked back to her car, and as she turned down the narrow aisle between her vehicle and the car parked next to her, a young man sitting in that adjacent car raised a shotgun from his lap and pointed it at her face.

I was switching back and forth between Oprah and Rosie, waiting for the news. I was nibbling on crackers and cheese, having a sip or two of wine. I was talking to the dogs, talking to the television, thinking about the day's work, thinking about tomorrow's work. At the same time, ten minutes from our house, four young men were threatening the life of the woman I love.

Three of them were in the car. The gunman sat in

the driver's seat. His vehicle was backed into the spot, ready to make his getaway. Two more sat in the rear seat, and suddenly in the aisle in front of her a fourth man appeared. He was large and baby-faced and wore a hat and an athletic jacket.

Apparently they had targeted her on one of her previous stops, followed her to the bookstore, parked their car next to hers, and readied their ambush. They'd positioned their car so that they were shielded from her view until she'd stepped deep into their trap.

When the gunman ordered her to throw down her purse, she complied immediately. And she threw down her car keys as well. This happened in seconds. Five, ten, fifteen. The big baby-faced youth scooped up her purse and the keys, and the gunman said, "Now you'll follow my instructions."

At home I was beginning to think she was running a little late. She's usually home by five. Anything later than five makes me start to prickle uneasily. It's an old habit. I'm a worrier. I know it's bad for my heart and blood pressure. I know I should stop being so obsessive. She's a grown woman, resolute and smart. She can take care of herself.

My wife had no way of knowing what the teenage gunman's instructions would be, but in that desperate moment for which she had utterly no preparation, she reached a clear and definite decision. She didn't wait for his command. She fled.

In her panic she chose to run around the building in the opposite direction from which she'd come. It was the longer of the two ways to the front door and the safety of the store, but somehow, despite her fright, instinctively she chose the best direction. Her going that way meant the gunman would have had to shoot through his own windshield if he wanted to fire after her. She made a brilliant and courageous choice, which very possibly saved her life. She ran and ran, and though it was only a few seconds, half a minute at the most, it was surely the most terrifying few moments of her life.

In the thousand times I have put myself in her position, I have made stupid choices every time. I have fantasized about saying something hostile to these guys. Or trying to wrestle the gun from the gunman's hand and turning it on him. Or I imagine being a wiseass—a character from one of my books—using my wit to befuddle them and talk my way out of danger. Or, more likely, I would have stood speechless, my bladder emptying.

In other words, I can't picture what I would have done. Because try as I might, I can't imagine her horror and anger and humiliation and panic and utter bewilderment. It is my occupation to imagine such things, but in this case my imagination utterly fails.

A few minutes later the phone in the kitchen rang.

The news anchors were reading their TelePrompTers, reciting much worse stories than this, urban crime at its most extreme, one outrage after the other. As always, the dozen or so narratives they'd selected for our evening viewing were electronically reduced, defanged, edited down to a few brisk television seconds—in other words, massively trivialized, made safe and bland for general consumption.

When the phone rang, I was watching the nightly

stream of crime. And because I had watched the same news the night before and the night before that and twenty-five years of night befores, I was distant and unmoved. If someone had questioned me at that moment concerning my attitudes about crime and its victims, I'm sure my answer would have been cynical and hard-bitten. After all, I've lived in the crime capital of America for over two decades. I've written about it, studied it, researched it. Offhand, I probably would have claimed that when it came to crime, nothing surprised me anymore.

I answered the phone. And I can hear her voice even now. Straining for air, trembling. Despite her own turmoil, her first words were chosen to comfort me. "I'm okay," she said. "I'm okay." But I was not comforted. Flares went off in my heart. "What happened? What is it?"

There was a police dispatcher on the line as well. In her good, efficient way this professional described what had happened to my wife and where she was. "You're sure you're all right?" I asked my wife. "You're not hurt?" "Yes, yes, I'm all right." But of course she was not all right. In some fundamental way she would never be all right again. And, in my own way, neither would I.

Either the dispatcher gave me the wrong location or in my panic I misheard. For I ran to my car, screamed through the neighborhood streets and across the highway, and tore into the parking lot of the wrong bookstore. I sprinted inside, found the manager. "Where's my wife?" I demanded. She thought I was joking, and she joked back, "I've got her tied up in the back office."

When we sorted out that monstrous miscommunication, she was aghast and deeply apologetic and went immediately to a phone and called the other bookstore and verified that my wife was there instead. I raced back to my car, sped through traffic, and arrived at the bookstore minutes later.

After the long embraces, the comforting words, and her torturous recitation of the events for police reports, we were home again. Numb with shock, we occupied ourselves with canceling credit cards and turning off the cell phone and the dozen other rituals of such post-traumatic moments.

The next day there was the welcome distraction of securing a new driver's license, a process that resulted in a stark and uncompromising ID photograph that for the next five years will bear constant witness to that desolate day.

Two days later the car was recovered. At the impound lot a worker asked me what had happened, and I told him the story of my wife's car-jacking, and he replied, "She was lucky. Not a day goes by we don't get a car in here with blood on the seats from someone who was wounded or murdered trying to defend their car." Lucky indeed.

On the way home I found a bullet in the ashtray and a CD in the player that was definitely not our music. I drove immediately to a car wash and paid for their premium service. But no vacuum or brush could clean away the psychic residues. The next weekend we sold the car.

The new car made only the smallest difference. Her innocence was shattered. And so was mine. Understandably, she battled anxiety. Things that had never frightened her began to push her to the edge of panic. For weeks even the most routine trips into the world were cause for deep uneasiness. And I struggled with my own anger and feelings of impotence. At that most crucial moment of our lives together, I had not been there to protect the woman I loved. And in the weeks afterward, no matter what I said or did, I could not penetrate to the core of her suffering.

In that fragile period there were also the less-than-sympathetic responses of friends who suggested that, since she hadn't been physically harmed, the whole event was little more than a bad scare. We bit our tongues and forgave them their lack of understanding. Fortunately, the justice system considered the event a great deal more serious than simply a scare, and when one of the perpetrators was finally caught, he was sentenced to a long stretch at Raiford.

When they heard her story, many of our friends and acquaintances had even worse stories to share. Mugged and pistol-whipped, car-jacked and kidnapped and held at gunpoint for hours. A south Florida catalog of misery. Rather than consoling us, as I'm sure they were meant to do, the sheer volume of similar or worse stories only served to reinforce our anxiety and mistrust of strangers. If you aren't safe at five in the afternoon in your front yard or a bookstore parking lot, where are you safe? If such a minor brush with crime can have such potent emotional consequences, what happens when the crime is a major one?

Six months later, at Christmas, by all outward appearances our lives were back to normal. She was shopping and running errands again. I was in the kitchen at five, nibbling and watching Oprah and Rosie. We could console ourselves in all the usual ways: There are a hundred crimes committed every day in our area that are far worse than this one. There was no bloodshed. The stolen merchandise was returned. One of the culprits caught. Yes, yes, yes, yes.

But even after half a year we didn't feel like a full-sized Christmas tree. Real celebration was out of the question. The wounds had not healed. And now, a year and a half later, they still haven't. As if on that dreary June afternoon, some essential tendon was torn inside our spirits. And even though it has mended now, both of us are still hobbled. We don't walk with the old bounce. The loss of security we suffered still echoes in every corner of our lives.

I have spent a good deal of my writing life describing the offenses men commit against one another, misdeeds many times more violent and extreme than this one. That my wife would become a victim in the parking lot of a bookstore is a profoundly unfunny irony.

Like most writers, I have worked hard to learn my craft so that it might carry the heaviest emotional freight I can manage to load it with. I try to write about the things that matter most, do justice to the crucial moments of my life and the lives of others, and I have long adhered to the belief that writing can bring both purgation and a deeper understanding of the most painful and difficult subjects.

But I am completely humbled by this event.

None of my sustaining artistic beliefs have sustained me here. There has been nothing purgative about recounting this episode. I understand this ugly incident and its repercussions not a bit better now than I did at the outset.

But then, as I suppose is true with injuries of every kind, Time is the only reliable medicine, forging on is the only cure. I know how paltry this bromide sounds, but at the moment, it's all the wisdom I can muster.

Perhaps by next Christmas, if we try very hard, we can add a foot or two to this year's tree.

WOODEN TENNIS RACKETS

When I first took up tennis in 1959, the racket I used was roughly the same size and shape as the rackets used in 1874 when Major Walter Clopton Wingfield first invented the game. In those eighty years the technology for making tennis rackets had evolved about as much as the technology for making baseball bats. Both were constructed in roughly the same manner and were shaped from exactly the same material that had always been used, wood.

Wood has many wonderful properties, not the least of which is that for centuries it was virtually the only cheap and abundant material that was light enough and durable enough and malleable enough to be shaped into objects as various as musical instruments, sailing ships, houses, furniture, and tennis rackets. There is also a magical and majestic quality to wood. The tree that was felled so that I might play tennis was once the home for hawks and owls. That tree might have shaded someone's home from the harsh summer sun or provided fruit for their table. It was a living thing that once towered above the earth and drew sustenance from deep below its surface.

None of this was of particular concern to me as a boy of twelve swatting at fuzzy balls and trying to learn the arcane method of scoring tennis. But I did appreciate the fact that because my tennis racket was wood, I could customize it. For my interest in tennis coincided with my passion for building model cars. When I wasn't on the tennis court, I worked long hours in the basement of my childhood home gluing together plastic car kits. But I wasn't content to merely follow the printed directions. No, I chopped and chanheled the bodies of those '32 Fords and cut corduroy to fit their interiors, a crude attempt to imitate rolled and pleated upholstery. I sanded the plastic bodies smooth, then applied layer after layer of candy-apple-red paint.

It seemed entirely natural to apply the same skills to my first tennis rackets. First I peeled away the bright plastic accent bands, then I began to sand away the name of whichever famous tennis player of that era, Pancho Gonzalez or Jack Kramer, was printed on my racket. I sanded and sanded and sanded until all that showed was the grain of the wood. Then I set about glopping on the wood stain. Finally, when the color was what I wanted, usually something dramatically dark, I varnished the wood to give it a gleaming, polished gloss.

When I was done, I had something totally unique and totally ludicrous. A one-of-a-kind racket that looked like a C-minus shop class project. But I swear I could serve better with some of those rackets than I can now. And I'm absolutely certain they sliced through the air with less friction than any of the space-age models of today. But most of all, I felt toward my racket an emotional attachment that I cannot begin to muster for my high-tech racket today.

When Pat Cash and John McEnroe met in the semi-finals of the U.S. Open in 1984, the match turned out to be the last time wooden rackets were used by both contestants in a major pro tournament. After that year wooden rackets quickly became an anachronism on the courts of America and continued to disappear rapidly until today the only place you can find a wooden racket is on display on the walls of stuffy tennis clubs or on the back shelves of antique stores.

When wooden rackets first began to vanish, there was a short period in which aluminum rackets were all the rage. I owned several gold and silver and green aluminum rackets in the late seventies, and though they were extremely lightweight and extremely stiff, aluminum's major virtue was that it never warped.

Warping was always a problem for wooden rackets, and every serious player owned a press for each of his rackets. You had to screw down each of the four wing nuts in the corners of the press until the trapezoid clamped tightly around the head of the racket and kept it rigidly flat. A press might not have been required in desert climates, but Florida's relentless humidity was very hard on wooden tennis rackets, as it is hard on all organic things. When I first began playing tennis in Florida I once forgot to use my press for a week or two, and the next time I pulled out my racket it was shaped like a spoon. Good for sifting sand but little else.

Now my racket is made of braided Kevlar. When I'm not using it to play tennis, I can always stuff it inside my shirt as body armor. No owls or hawks ever roosted in the stuff that comprises my racket. In fact, before this thing was a tennis racket, it didn't exist. It was merely a combination of exotic chemicals concocted in a lab somewhere, then poured molten into molds shaped like tennis rackets. After the rackets cooled and were removed from the mold, the naked Kevlar was spray-painted the newest, raciest, Day-Gloiest, highest rated market-tested colors yet devised, and finally it was given a pulse-shaking, lapel-grabbing name like Hammer or Revelation.

Pete Sampras uses a Kevlar racket, or one made of fiberglass or graphite or some other material that only Pete can afford. Because the materials in his racket have been artificially created with power in mind, Pete's serve and the serves of a few other men on the pro tennis tour are so powerful that these days it is becoming increasingly difficult to watch a professional tennis match without the aid of special optical gear.

And power is not the only thing these high-tech fibers generate. The new rackets also have a much larger sweet spot than ever before. The sweet spot is that place on the racket's strings where the optimum trampoline effect occurs. In the old days with wooden rackets, the sweet spot was about the size of a dime. If the ball made contact with the strings outside that dime-sized zone, the dull thud that resulted sent shock waves up the arm and turned the elbow into a tuning fork. And where the ball went after such an off-center hit was anyone's guess.

These days the sweet spot is huge. With an oversized racket, even a beginner with faulty eyesight playing in pitch-dark conditions is virtually guaranteed to find the sweet spot.

The purist in me disdains such "improvements," while the failing, fading, gimpy, increasingly geriatric side of me celebrates anything that extends my tennis life a few years longer.

But overall, I miss the wood.

A few weeks back I actually took my old Dunlop Maxply out of its press and went to the courts to whack a few. This racket was the same model used by Rod Laver to win two grand slams, a feat not accomplished since. The Dunlop Maxply was once considered the Ferrari of tennis rackets, a sensitive little tiger that could generate power without losing the feel of the ball on the strings. It had touch and control and smashing strength. But after years of using my braided Kevlar racket, the old wood had a dull, lethargic feel. I managed to get a few balls over the net, but the concentration required to keep the ball in the exact center of the strings of that tiny racket with its tiny sweet spot is beyond me these days. As much as I'd like to romanticize those old wooden rackets, they simply don't have the oomph that most tennis players have come to expect of their weapons.

Nevertheless, I feel about my old wooden rackets the same way I feel about my old manual Underwood typewriter. Toiling with those sticky keys, banging the carriage back to the left at the end of each line, as well

as all that backbreaking athletic labor that I per-
formed for decades with my wooden tennis rackets,
has made me eternally grateful for the ease with
which the words now unspool beneath my fingers,
and for the effortless grace with which the balls fly off
my strings.

DRIPPING CLOCKS

It's been over thirty years since I first made acquaintance with the shuffleboard capital of the world, Saint Petersburg, Florida. Back in the mid-sixties I spent four rollicking years there as a college student. Then a few years later on, I migrated back to Saint Pete and took the only job I could find, shoveling dirt for a landscaping company. For most of a year, along with a handful of other out-of-work Ph.D.s, I tested myself against the unyielding sun and stubborn soil of that quaint and quiet Gulf Coast town.

Now when I go back to Saint Pete, as I did recently, I take great pleasure in pointing out the palm trees that I planted so many lifetimes ago. Several of those trees are on Saint Pete Beach, and they shade the parking lots of a half-dozen of the towering condominiums that with tedious uniformity line nearly every inch of the coast. The palms are thirty years older now, and their shadows have lengthened considerably, but in the last three decades, while the rest of Florida boomed, those shadows are nearly all that's changed in Saint Pete.

The Gulf is still as tranquil as a lake, and the beach is wide and littered with a daily dose of seashells. Old folks with rolled-up pants still scrutinize the damp shoreline, then stoop and pluck, filling their net bags with pounds of the dead crustaceans. As far as I can tell, the demographics are the same: midwesterners predominate, sweatshirts from Indiana and Michigan and Ohio leading the way. And even though thirty years have passed, apparently the average age of beachgoers on Saint Pete Beach has not dipped by so much as a year. Holding steady at seventy-seven.

Downtown, Webb City, the world's largest and silliest drugstore, is gone, replaced by interstates and a new and rarely used arena. But dear, sweet, goofy Sunken Gardens is still charming tourists with "Kachuga & the Alligator" shows. And for the true explorer, there is as always Sunken Gardens' "mile long adventure path."

I was overjoyed to find that the two best outdoor beer joints in this part of the galaxy are still pumping out the greasiest, most delicious cheeseburgers anywhere. Ted Peters is located on the beach, while the Chattaway can be found by simply sniffing the air anywhere near downtown.

Or if you prefer quieter entertainments, you can dawdle on the famous green benches that are planted every ten feet in the dead center of downtown Saint Pete. Just as they were thirty years ago, those green benches are nearly always occupied by a drowsy group of senior citizens who are no doubt exhausted from a rousing game of shuffleboard.

In my callous college days, we made great sport of

these somnolent white-haired citizens. There was even a competition among the most heartless of us to see how many strokes or heart attacks or fainting spells we could witness in a year's time. The old folks were fair game because of the great gulf of years between us. Comic targets for a generation that was going to stay young forever.

But on a recent sunny afternoon in midwinter, as I sat among them happily, I felt a sudden yawning ache in my throat, a time-warp sense of being in two different halves of my life at once, stranded awkwardly between youth and old age. As I watched, my younger self walked by and shot me a ghostly sneer, and I was struck with an odd blend of melancholy and terror, a sentimental Irish swoon that more and more lately has taken me by surprise. It was a feeling of utter dislocation, as though my very synapses and neurons were suddenly uncertain whether this was the middle of the century or the end of it.

It was a surreal feeling. Out of body. The way it must feel to be beamed aboard the Enterprise. For a millisecond that seemed to last forever, my body was both places at once.

This is the strange magic of Saint Petersburg. The town that time forgot. Where the moss still hangs from the oaks like wisps of fog, where the old majestic hotels, the Don CeSar and the Vinoy, have been reborn into perfect replicas of themselves, and where one local museum's walls are covered by the absurd, timeless paintings of Salvador Dali.

What, you might ask, are such Dali masterpieces as *The Hallucinogenic Toreador* or *Slave Market with the*

Disappearing Bust of Voltaire doing in the shuffle-board capital of America? Well, it's a long story, which began when an industrialist from Ohio and his wife were first spellbound by Dali's work in the 1940s. They went on to befriend Dali and his wife and to devote much of their lives to collecting Dali's work. And when they decided to donate their vast collection of treasures to a tourist-oriented community, somehow Saint Pete shouldered to the front of the line.

The museum occupies a low concrete bunker about equidistant from the gorgeous twinkling bay and the Bayfront Auto Repair shop, a bustling place housed in a rusty corrugated building. It's a part of town that Realtors usually describe as "transitional," though in this case it is not yet clear where that transit is headed. Whichever way it goes, the one sure thing is that it won't get there quick. Nothing in Saint Pete does.

There was no line at the museum the day I went. A high school group was gawking at some of the more graphic depictions of surreal sexual apparatuses; otherwise the place was empty except for me and the armed guards who lurked around every switchback. The place is run by grandmothers, kindly women who that morning seemed genuinely excited to tout their latest exhibit, which presented some important moments in Dali's adventures in advertising. On the walls there were ludicrous and outrageous advertisements for hosiery, lipstick, and perfume published in *Vogue,* an album cover for Jackie Gleason's *Lonesome Echo* album, a travel poster for a railroad line. It's a dizzying display of the tasteful, the distasteful, and the tasteless. Dali selling Jackie Gleason?

Though the museum has been open for sixteen years, it seems brand-new, barely used, in that way that well-maintained public buildings often are. On the other hand, with its nondescript architecture and its resolutely unflashy style, the place seems ageless, ahistorical, as if the designers had been too shy to let on what a flamboyant spectacle awaited you inside.

In a strange and wonderful way, it's a perfect match. Saint Pete and Dali. Two ageless charmers who felt no need to conform to the raucous mutations of modern life but instead held resolutely to their own goofy drumbeats, their own outlandish visions of normalcy.

Bully for them.

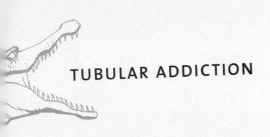

TUBULAR ADDICTION

In his book *Creating from the Spirit,* my friend Dan Wakefield describes the sinister power of television. "A few months after I gave up TV, I found myself turning the tube back on in that automatic way, sinking back into the habit, the numbness. Like all other addictions, this one isn't beat just because you conquer it once. It creeps right back into your life and takes over. It's a serious drug, a narcotic of mind and soul."

Had I read this before a trip I took to the mountains of North Carolina, I would have said Dan was balmy, some kind of anticulture snob who worries too much. But after ten days of living in a primitive cabin deprived of television, I've come to fully accept Dan's view. If anything, he might have underestimated the seductiveness of this particular opiate.

For the few days that my parents joined my wife and me in that spartan Carolina cabin, without the endless drone of the college bowl games to distract us, we were forced for the first time in my adult life to participate in sustained conversations. The results were astonishing. After an initial awkwardness in the spacious silence of those hours together, my father began to discuss his war experiences fifty years earlier. I'd always felt deprived because he hadn't shared more of that gut-wrenching time, and now, without the babble of television to divert us, he opened up. In those two or three days, I learned more about my father's life before I was born than I had heard in all the years before. His stories were moving and vivid and helped illuminate a man I had long wished to know better. Even my mother, married for over fifty years, was surprised to discover things my father had withheld from her all that time.

Of course, some of his willingness to speak might have been precipitated by other things. The good wine I'd brought along, for instance, or our advancing ages, which compel us to finally speak the words we might not get the chance to speak again. But I think the intimacy we discovered in those hours was due primarily to the absence of television. With nothing to distract us, we quickly wore out the trifling family news, the gossip, and our views on O. J. Simpson and began to root around through the deeper layers of personal remembrance and filial concern.

With no television jangling in the corner of the room, we looked to each other for our amusements and were rewarded with a closeness and warmth that was long overdue. After a few days of such visceral talk and a week and a half of calming quiet, I was determined to add to my short list of New Year's resolutions a disavowal of television.

I switched the set off and was determined to keep it

off, to extend for as long as possible the serene dispo-
sition I had brought back with me to south Florida. I
never suspected how difficult it would be to keep
such a pledge. For I had never actually added up
before the number of hours I let the television mum-
ble on. And when I finally did the math, the facts were
stunning.

Ever susceptible to addiction, I had fallen into the
habit of switching on the tube in the morning when I
woke at five o'clock, so I could immediately begin
catching up on the parade of atrocities and outrages
that had occurred overnight, and so I could continue
to follow the ongoing investigations of the other atrocities and outrages that had happened yesterday and
the day before. Somehow I had made a special place
in my own cultural snobbery for television news, a
more generous dispensation of viewing time than I
would ever consider squandering on sitcoms or soaps.
As the years passed I had gradually added the *Today*
show or *Good Morning America* as quasi-news pro-
grams that would further help me stay abreast of the
national atrocities and outrages.

So that on an average day, by the time I was ready to
retreat to my office and begin my workday, the television had gabbled away for several hours. At lunch
there was the noon news, a half hour, sometimes an
hour, so I could fully familiarize myself with any new
atrocities that had occurred in the three hours since
breakfast. On most days, shockingly, there seemed to
be many.

Then it was back to work, with a small transitional
period of buzzing brain from the caffeine of television

news. At four I had fallen into the habit of wandering back into the house to see if Rosie or Oprah were interviewing any authors or other intellectuals who might give me some revelation about the meaning of life. Somehow, in my addictive derangement, I had smuggled talk shows into the quasi-news category. Of course, Rosie or Oprah are almost always interviewing movie stars who are plugging their latest, or an expert in dysfunctional marriages or dysfunctional eating or some other newly discovered dysfunction. (Though you never see them deal with television addiction.) And the talk shows were followed by a full two hours of local, national, late-breaking, and live accounts of even more outrages and atrocities.

After adding it up, I was appalled to find that in my pre–primitive cabin period, I frequently devoted more hours of the day to watching news than I did to my writing career. Without realizing it, I had taken on a virtual second job.

Of course, in my defense, for most of those hours of news, I was not exactly engrossed in the stories. The chatter between the television personalities naturally takes up much of that time, and there are many minutes when my attention is turned to other matters while the television gabbles on. And clearly, with so much exposure to the atrocities and outrages of the world, I was far better prepared to invent my own fictional atrocities and outrages.

But so many hours of television news is, by any standard, an enormous waste, a ceaseless clamor that holds real thought and real conversation hostage to the next surge of noise, the next breaking story. This just in!

The good news is that in facing the monstrous pro-portion of my TV news addiction, I have taken the first large step on the road to recovery. I am now fully pre-pared to be a less well-informed guy, not to have on the tip of my tongue the names of the latest preteen shooting victims, not even to know the exact dollar figure that O. J. is worth or how much reparation he must pay to his victims' families. Only a few days have gone by since I severely limited my news intake, and already I feel wonderfully liberated, hugely ill informed.

Now I must begin the next and most difficult phase of my recovery, to summon all my strength and self-discipline so that I can face my really serious addic-tion: TV sports.

APRIL IS THE CRUELEST MONTH

Call me crazy, but I must admit I don't mind filing my income tax. In fact, it has always given me a certain crude pleasure to tidy up my year's accounts, adding all those columns of figures, digging around in this year's shoebox clogged with receipts, deciphering ingenious notes I made to myself in July about why a vacation to Sanibel Island was a necessary tax-deductible business trip. When I'm finished and all the math has been computed accurately and all the numbers have found their correct places on the neat white form, there's a sweet relief, the kind of intense satisfaction I understand that certain compulsives feel after alphabetizing all their CDs or arranging each and every shirt in their closet according to the international color scale.

But year after year that satisfaction is cruelly short-lived. For immediately after I'm finished totaling all the expenses, like some self-lacerating idiot, I shrug off last year's resolution never to repeat this act again, and I stare at the ugly truth of exactly how much I spent this year on video rentals.

Before I even begin to register what this number signifies about my own failed budgetary discipline, I am struck dumb by wonder at Wayne Huizinga's decision to swap his video rental business for the car trade. I, for one, could buy two Coupe de Villes and a used KIA on what I spent last year on bad movies.

Oh, but there was a logic to it at the time. An eternal hopefulness as well.

In a typical weekly foray to the movie store, I wander the aisles aimlessly, unable to recall a single title that's been recommended to me lately. I am the perfect customer, a bundle of wild impulses, eager to fill the void of my Friday night with a feast of empty calories. I want to zone out on visual pizza. I want a cheap and legal high, a deep snort of popular culture.

While passing down the thriller aisle, I am immediately seized by the steamy photo on a box, a woman draped in a classic seductive pose around the torso of a man who, my god, looks a great deal like me. Of course, I have no choice but to take down the movie and weigh its possibilities as my night's entertainment.

As I read the fine-print blurbs, I repeat the silent mantra that leads me again and again to commit these foolish acts. Just because I've never heard of *Hepcat in Vegas* doesn't automatically mean it's a dud. Surely there were some very good movies made in the last year or so that played in theaters without grabbing my attention. Maybe *Hepcat in Vegas* was one of those. So what if I've never heard of any of the actors? When I first saw *Easy Rider* I'd never heard of Jack Nicholson or Dennis Hopper. And what about *Body Heat*? When I saw it for the first time Kathleen Turner and William

Hurt were as unknown to me as Adolph Mozzarella and Glendia Jackson-Spearmint, the stars of *Hepcat in Vegas*.

But even as I tuck the movie under my arm, somewhere in the darkest reaches of my unconscious I know that this is more than likely going to be a wretched film, one that I'll eject within the first five minutes. Having been disappointed so often in the past, however, only fuels this weekly feeding frenzy. For I must rent not only one potential loser but a backup, and possibly a third alternative as well, just in case. So I forge on, gripping *Hepcat* with mindless optimism, searching out numbers two and three.

At home the bitter truth is soon apparent. *Hepcat* is worse than a dud. It was written and directed by a maniacal eight-year-old with the moral vision and attention span of a newly hatched mosquito. The actors are so miserable they would flub as extras in a Super Bowl crowd. And I shudder to confess that the biggest dolt of all is the actor I thought looked like me.

The conventional wisdom among screenwriters and other Hollywood types is that audiences must find the screen characters sympathetic and engaging within the first ten minutes of a film or you've lost them. Fortunately, *Hepcat in Vegas* didn't require the full ten. Two was plenty.

Another $4.95 to add to the long column of fiscal irresponsibility.

But ah, look, there on the coffee table are movie number two and movie number three, throbbing with possibilities. So like a good film rental citizen, I dutifully rewind *Hepcat,* pop it out, slip in number two, fast-forward past ten minutes of previews of movies that seem to be written and directed and acted by even younger and more maniacal children, and as number two begins to roll, I realize that from sheer blind luck I have managed to select a film that, while I would never have paid eight dollars to see it in a movie theater, is not so abysmally bad that I must eject it immediately. Thirty minutes later, I am asleep on the couch.

Thus begins phase two of this frightful scenario. Saturday and Sunday are devoured by social events and catching up on the week's errands. Stocking up on rawhide chewies for the dogs, crucial stuff like that. All the while, movie number two is lodged in the VCR slot with its meter ticking silently. As I pass back and forth through the living room all weekend, I glance guiltily at the VCR. I always intend to watch the rest of that movie. For after all, it is not abysmal. But come Sunday night, as the *60 Minutes* gang executes its weekly tomahawk journalism, movie number two is still sleeping within the machine.

Here is the moment when a thrifty, provident, judicious individual would rewind the unwatched flick and get in the car and drive back to the movie store and slide that waste of good money into the all-night return bin. But who among us really feels like driving in the dark of a dreary Sunday night to a store ten blocks away merely to save $4.95? Weary from that weekend of errands and house cleaning, I let it slide.

And then, of course, the whirlwind of the week comes, and *Hepcat in Vegas* and its noble brother and sister sit on the coffee table collecting dust and ring-

ing up charges. From the looks of my year-end column of figures, I would estimate that on average I return those films on Wednesday, just before I get the ominous call from the movie rental store to remind me their priceless films are missing and that I am about to be presumed dead. So that in the end, after skillfully faking myself out in a dozen different ways, I find I have paid twice as much as I might have in a theater for movies I would never have gone to see on the big screen in the first place.

When, except at tax time, are we forced to confront so starkly the exact expense of our slothfulness and dissipation? I'm no longer sure the pleasure of tidying up my ledgers balances out against the discomfort of facing such waste. Maybe it's time to begin thinking about an accountant.

CLOSE ENCOUNTER

I know it doesn't sound like much, sitting out in your backyard for two hours, doing nothing, just observing whatever shows up. But that's the assignment I gave my students this week. They were reading *Walden,* Thoreau's account of his more than two *years* of woodsy contemplation in Concord, Massachusetts, and I thought such a task might give them a tiny glimpse of what Thoreau experienced.

Almost from the first moment when I decided to accept this challenge myself, I began to stall, finding innumerable excuses to delay serving this two-hour sentence. Letters to write, bills to pay, e-mail to answer, and several household projects to complete. There is, of course, always something to fritter away your time on, always some distraction available to those trying to dodge contemplation.

I also found myself thinking a lot about the approaching two hours of forced passivity. No writing implements, no book to read, no CNN, no cursor pulsing on the screen. Would I even be able to manage it, to sit still and just look and listen and observe for two hours? So it was with more than a little dread that I took my seat out in the gazebo, fearing that I did not have the meager inner resources to handle such a dose of idleness and quiet.

I needn't have worried, for when I eased back into the chair, I was immediately struck by the noise and activity around me. My acre of earth is at least a mile away from the nearest busy two-lane road, but the ocean roar of that roadway was as clear and definite as if I were sitting along its shoulder. Nor am I in the flight path of any major airport, yet within seconds I heard the deep rumble of a passing jet, and in the following few minutes there were at least four more, as well as a small prop plane flying low overhead. Its fifteen seconds of tumult resonated through the timbers of the gazebo and blotted out the twittering of jays and cardinals and mockingbirds. But that was not all. For in the next block someone was using an early morning chain saw, and for the next hour its savage roar provided a constant accompaniment for my meditation.

Scientists call this phenomenon The Great Hum and say that modern American life is profoundly afflicted by these man-made vibrations that quietly but insistently ruffle the silence. In fact, they say, the natural world is so thoroughly polluted by noise that it is virtually impossible to spend more than fifteen minutes anywhere in the lower forty-eight without hearing the throb of a motor. If this is so, then surely all that jangling of the cerebral cortex has some deleterious effects. Surely The Great Hum is partly to blame for the jittery pace of modern life, the constantly accelerating rush to get from point A to point B, and the intolerance for dawdlers. No doubt this low-grade white noise seeps into the very marrow and sets up a numbing purr.

Motors, motors everywhere and not a thought to think.

The first hour whizzed by. I sat, I observed. Everywhere I looked around the yard, I saw another project that needed completing. For I was not sitting in the wilderness of Thoreau's Walden Pond but on tamed land, a suburban simulated forest where nearly every tree and shrub bore some sign of my clippers or saw blade. Though I prefer an undomesticated look to my greenery, good sense continually reminds me that I must strip the vines from the hibiscus or it will soon be all vines and no pink flowers. And I must trim the trees back from their natural lushness or risk losing them in the next big wind.

Thoreau had the luxury to be a non-interventionist. Since he was not a caretaker, he could simply sit back and observe and enjoy the unruliness of nature. But because ownership begets a measure of responsibility, this small parcel of nature is not a purely natural place. Instead, it is my ongoing project, a reflection of my needs and my notions of beauty. Though I have not gone so far as to shape my hedges into the topiary forms of jumping dolphins, I *have* evened their edges. I make them into boxes, civilizing them, taming their wildness. Though I know this is a necessary act if I don't want to see the whole yard strangled by vines and mangy shrubs, yet some liveliness and sparkle seems lost in all this hacked and trimmed and tightly managed green space.

As my second hour is winding down, I am vaguely disappointed that I have had no transcendent encounters. No stately osprey circled overhead. No angelic flock of ibises fluttered onto my lawn. As close as I've come to a truly inspirational moment was a few minutes earlier when a neighbor's two-ton air-conditioning unit shut off and the relative silence was astounding.

I am almost ready to call it quits and return to the blinking cursor and check my phone messages when I notice an insect walking along the arm of my chair. It's sandy-colored, no bigger than a pencil point. It is translucent, so inconsequential I could smush it with a careless gesture and not even register the moment. On closer inspection I see that the tiny bug is tottering along unsteadily, lugging some large coiled apparatus on its back. Is he carrying a trophy, or some kind of food, or perhaps another of his kind wounded on the field of battle? Or perhaps he is engaged in some blissful state of union with his female counterpart. The creature is so small, I would need a powerful magnifier to tell if this is two creatures conjoined or just a single bug with a very tall and unwieldy hat.

For several moments it wanders aimlessly, staggering under its load, meandering back and forth beside my arm, making ticklish explorations of my flesh, evaluating this gigantic interloper as friend or foe or potential food. He seems to be in no particular hurry. Certainly not intimidated by me. He's just prowling across my land as if he owned it. A smug little bug in no rush to complete the job he has to do.

So that is as close to an epiphany as I'm going to get today. A brief encounter with some nameless, nearly invisible critter, bizarrely shaped and glowing with otherworldly light, as fragile as a soap bubble. I watch it trek away across the Everest of my chair, moving forward with utter serenity and purpose. More at home in this place and more the owner of this land than I will ever be.

HOT DAMN!

My first brush with greatness was at sixteen, when I played a tennis match against a kid three years my junior. I was a senior in high school, and because tennis was not yet the showbiz sport it is today, I didn't recognize the kid's name and had no way to know he was ranked nationally. I held the number one spot on my prep school's tennis team and had illusions that I might one day play world-class tennis, although in those days I'd never seen world-class tennis and truly had no way to measure my ability except to look in the one tattered copy of *World Tennis Magazine* I owned. Yes, I thought, my strokes vaguely resembled Rod Laver's, so maybe there was hope. But on that afternoon in the spring of 1965, I played this kid who was three years younger, and he beat me 6–0, 6–0 and was noticeably bored for most of the match. Some ten years later I watched him in the finals at Wimbledon. He lost that day, but it was a good match, and only then did I realize that this was the kid with a goofy name who had cleaned my clock a decade before.

Like all my subsequent brushes with greatness,

this one took a familiar turn. The kid was absolutely unprepossessing. He was normal. Less than normal. Ordinary. Personally unmemorable. He did one thing that was very good. He played tennis. He hit his serves with a pace so blinding I barely got my strings on one of them all day. He sent the ball to places on the court where I'd never seen a tennis ball go before. He didn't miss. He seemed never to hurry. But at the net when he shook my hand, he was utterly normal. A ninth grader. A kid with pimples, gawky and ill at ease. Not the least bit cocky. Just a great player with his eyes on the far horizon. Looking way past me.

A few years later at a summer camp in upstate New York, I joined the other basketball counselors in a game arranged by the camp's owner, who happened to be a friend of the coach of the New York Knicks. That August afternoon the whole camp turned out to witness a game between the Knicks and the hicks. Of course, we didn't come close. They moved so fast and were so tall, it was all a blur. At halftime, Walt Frazier challenged all five of our starters to steal the ball from him. He dribbled inside the center jump circle, and we stood outside the circle and tried to snare the ball. Ten reasonably quick hands stabbing at his dribble. No one touched it. We looked awfully silly. Like five guys trying to snatch a piece of mist.

Although I know that any great athlete's abilities are the result of some wonderful fusion of natural gifts and tireless drilling, there seems to be something almost magical about the quicker-than-the-eye elegance of a Michael Jordan or Serena Williams. And as with all magic, we can't help suspecting that there's a gimmick at work, some trick behind the illusion. And this is probably why many of us resist admitting athletes into the inner circle of greatness. For after all, isn't it just their bodies that are great? Their timing, their coordination, their strength and endurance. Oh, sure, great athletes must have the depth of character, the gristle and stubborn willingness to endure difficulties, and the determination to focus all their being on the performance of their sport. And yes, a great athletic performance can send our hearts soaring. Still, I for one can't quite equate greatness in sport to some of the other forms of greatness I've encountered.

I met James Dickey three times. The first occasion was just after his book of poetry *Buckdancer's Choice* had been selected for a National Book Award. At that time, in the small arena of literary eminence, there was no one hotter. I was a college student, an aspiring poet, and I sat enraptured in the audience and watched Dickey perform. When he stopped in the middle of the long narrative poem "Cherrylog Road," and lifted his face to the audience and said, "Hot damn! I forgot how good that poem was," the audience murmured its approval and fell into a swoon. What a moment! A great poet was having a powerful surge of feeling right before my eyes. A major American writer was genuinely enjoying this evening while reading a poem that just happened to be the best poem I'd ever read.

Years later, I sat in another audience at a writers conference and listened to Dickey read again. At exactly the same spot in "Cherrylog Road" he stopped and looked up at the audience. His face was shining. He was sweating with excitement and drink. "Hot damn!" he exclaimed. "I forgot how good that poem was." My heart failed. I slumped down in my seat, bereft, utterly disillusioned, while all around me the other writers and students fell into the same swoon I'd enjoyed years before.

Toward the end of his life, I saw Dickey read at a university. I listened with dread as he approached the fateful line in "Cherrylog Road." And yes, once again, it was "Hot damn!" And all the rest. The audience murmured, enraptured at this seemingly special moment. And I sat still, thinking of greatness, how it is composed of so many parts. There is the greatness of the writer who labors alone in a room to bring forth an arrangement of language that surpasses language, words that become an incantation, a prayer from the deepest layers of self, but somehow transcend self and can wake in others that same transcendence. "Cherrylog Road" is that kind of poem.

But there is another kind of greatness too. The greatness of the performer, of the orator, of the silver-tongued mesmerizer. Dickey could read his poems with the overripe, oratorical plushness they deserved. But for some reason he decided he needed to go a little bit further, to resort to this cheap theatrical trick, and as if that were not bad enough, he did not have the wit or energy to vary his routine over the course of several decades.

And then there was Dickey's social self, which I witnessed on several occasions. He was monumentally boorish, a drunk, a blatant womanizer, a rude and sloppy man. He was also very funny and could rouse himself to great heights of storytelling, though these narratives were usually at the expense of another writer or academic. In short, Dickey was one of a breed of writers, a large tribe, I'm sorry to report, who have apparently put the best of themselves into their work and have little left over for their real life. We have so many notorious examples of great writers who were tragic and pitiful creatures in their privates lives— from Hemingway and Fitzgerald to Sylvia Plath and Anne Sexton and a host of other writers who committed suicide in one form or another—that it has unfortunately become part of the job description of the American writer: to be considered a great American writer, you must be a deeply flawed, agonized soul, constantly teetering on the edge of self-destruction. The idea is one of those leftover Romantic notions that still bedevils many who are considering a career in the arts. "I don't think I'm sufficiently tortured to be a great writer," a student said to me once. "Yes," I said. "Maybe you should consider another direction."

I met a Kennedy once. A male Kennedy. I was attending a fund-raiser where he was the guest speaker. The cause was environmental, but the small group attending seemed more interested in brushing shoulders with a Kennedy than in saving trees and birds. I hung around on the edge of a group who were chatting with the young man. He seemed shy, slightly ill at ease. But there was that loose and easy Kennedy smile, that haircut, those rangy good looks. I guess the others in the group had set their charisma-ometers too high, because when Kennedy was called away to the phone, several of the folks agreed that while this guy was clearly from the Kennedy gene pool, he was no Jack.

Shakespeare said, "Some are born great, some achieve greatness, and some have greatness thrust upon them." Well, as this young Kennedy took his place at the head of the room and began to speak, it was immediately clear that he met all three criteria. He spoke about nature, about its importance in America's history, about the difficulty that men of good conscience have when faced with choices between preserving the natural world and preserving jobs. He quoted poets, he quoted law and history, he quoted the words of ordinary citizens, he gave us statistics, and he gave us lyricism. He was more than simply eloquent, more than simply right. For half an hour he was Walt Frazier, dribbling faster than the eye could see. He was Michael Jordan, hanging near the rim with gravity-defying grace. He was James Dickey, generating the incandescent white heat of words. And he was the ordinary guy we'd been unimpressed with a few minutes earlier, only now he was a man possessed. He was Orpheus, and we were the birds charmed down from the branches of our tree. This young man had transformed himself before our eyes into something so rare, so inspirational, so amazing, that it was both stirring and humbling at once. He was no longer a Kennedy. He was simply one of us. No more, no less. But he was also our best self, that person we feel lurking down there in our beings just out of sight, yearning for release. For a moment his eloquence summoned that part of me to life, and I felt truly exalted. The fairy dust of greatness was everywhere. The room was twinkling with it. It's still twinkling.

Hot damn!

LETTER TO MY FATHER

Dear Daddy-O:

I write this now on the day you died. Writing is the only act I can manage at the moment, the only way I know to deal with the ache of grief and loss. I suppose I've learned to handle my pain this way because, like you, I've never been one to openly display my emotions.

In fact, the only time I ever saw you cry was that afternoon when you came walking back with the .22 rifle in your hand after putting our dog Richie out of his misery. It was a powerful moment, one that I reminded you of a few weeks ago as I sat beside your bed and we had what we both knew was our final conversation. I told you then that I was grateful to have had a father who cried after shooting the family pet. I expect there were many kids in my town back then whose fathers would have been unmoved by such a chore, who would have come walking back to the house with the same stoic look they wore when they left. I'm glad I had you as my model, strong enough to do what needed to be done yet vulnerable enough for tears.

It's strange what we remember. Strange that among the thousands of moments we shared, a certain handful give shape to my memory of you. I remember you diving off the low board at Kentucky Lake. You did a better-than-average swan dive, but jackknifes were your specialty. I don't remember any other adults diving except you. Mostly it was kids doing cannonballs or watermelons or belly flops. It wasn't that your jackknife was so graceful. It was stiff and formal, a little hokey. I guess I was slightly embarrassed that you were doing it at all. But it strikes me now as marvelous that you would overcome your shyness to bounce on that springy board and arc upward and bend and touch your toes, then straighten out again in time to slice into the water—not to show off, not to give your sons a memory they would cherish forever, but because it so obviously felt good to do that dive, because it made you feel beautiful and alive, all the parts of your body still working harmoniously, still muscular and elastic.

Aside from diving, your other main athletic interest was your long flirtation with body-building machines. There were many over the years, but I remember one with particular clarity. A three-foot rod with red wooden handles and some sort of rubber-coated elastic spring in the middle. The object was to bend the bar into a U and make the handles touch. To build your pectoral muscles. You had wonderful pectoral muscles, Daddy-O. And your arms and hands were stronger than any I've ever known. I remember you saying once, when I was bragging about how many push-ups I'd done, that the important thing to remember about exercise was never to stop. Because once you stopped, it was hard to get going again. I was four-teen at the time, which would have made you about ten years younger than I am right now. Well, I want you to know, Daddy, I did forty push-ups this morning, on this day they withdrew your ventilator and stepped away from your bed. I haven't stopped. I won't stop. I promise you that.

You took me shooting a few times along the banks of Little River. We used that same .22 to shoot beer cans off stumps, to plink at things floating in the water. Not real hunting, just target practice. Tramping through the woods beside you, carrying a rifle through the raw Kentucky autumn, I remember your lessons in how to carry a firearm, how to aim it, how to squeeze the trigger. But most vividly I recall the maxim you shared with me as I was bulling mindlessly through the woods. "Don't step on anything you can step over," you said. You learned that in the war. You were a mine sweeper. Then you told me the only war story you ever shared, about an impatient officer who ignored your order not to drive his Jeep down the snow-covered road that you and your team had not yet swept for mines. He made it a hundred yards before he and his Jeep were blown to pieces. "Don't step on anything you can step over." At the time I took it literally to mean that I should avoid the logs, the rocks, anything I didn't recognize. Years later, I thought the saying must have some larger metaphorical significance. A warning to avoid strife and confrontation, to go around rather than through the rough patches. But now your phrase echoes in my head as simple wis-dom. "Step carefully through the world. Be aware."

When I came home to say my final good-bye, I spent

the day beside your bed and watched you enter and leave your dream state. Your hands moved through the air, pantomiming your reveries. In one of them, you reached out and plucked something that floated before you and brought it to your mouth, and then you began to pat your chest with both hands. Mother asked you what you were doing, and you opened your eyes and looked at her dreamily and said, "Strawberry." You had picked the delicious red fruit from the vaporous bush before you and brought it to your parched lips, and then you must have assumed it had fallen from your fingers because you tasted nothing. Later on that day, we brought you a real strawberry, and you put it in your mouth and said in your hoarse, breathless voice, "Very sweet."

After your final operation, the drugs gave you mild hallucinations. At first you saw disturbing things appearing on the wall across from your bed, and when Mother asked you what you were seeing, you said it was handwriting. She asked you what the handwriting said, and you told her that it was a list of people's names. It was as if you were seeing in that handwriting on the wall the invisible traces of all those people who had come before you. Finding your own place among the endless list of names. An image both unnerving and comforting, a poetic rendering of what you surely felt approaching.

Once when your condition turned grim and you were banished again into the ceaseless brightness and mayhem of the ICU, you instructed Mother to go home and get the Mustang convertible and bring it to the hospital because you wanted to ride home with the top down. Years ago you won that Mustang convertible, first prize in a contest you entered. It was just another of your goofy postretirement hobbies, entering sweepstakes, contests of every kind. Often inserting my name or my brother's. There was one lucky time when through your efforts I was the proud recipient of a hamburger maker, a popcorn machine shaped like Conestoga wagon, and a plastic picnic set, all of them won in the course of one week.

That in the depths of your illness you fantasized about driving home from the hospital with the top down, basking in the beautiful spring weather, seems to me perfect testimony to your playful spirit, your joy in natural pleasures, your whimsy. Even in the midst of the horrors of those final days, you knew, by god, what would delight you most.

It is a commonplace for men of my generation to complain that they never received their father's complete and unequivocal blessing. They never heard their father say that simple phrase "I'm proud of you, of who you've become." Well, I'm happy to report that you, as naturally reticent as you were, managed to let me know in countless ways how proud you were of me.

I recall the mischievous pleasure you took in describing how you had repositioned my books on a grocery store shelf so they were more prominently displayed at eye level. An act that earlier in your life you might have considered a form of vandalism. I cherish the letter you wrote after finishing one of my novels, in which you described what had become your normal reading practice. You gulped the book down as fast as you could to find out what happened, then you read it slowly a second time to savor all the little things you missed the first time through. You were my perfect reader, Dad. My absolute perfect reader.

You practiced your own art in those marvelous wood carvings. It started out as simple whittling to pass the slow hours around the real estate office. At first you focused on the usual tricks. A long chain of interlocking walnut links. A ball that rattled around behind the bars of a wood box. But you moved on in the last few years to birds and fish and flowers and intricate tableaux of hillbilly silliness. A moonshiner stumbling over his own feet, jug in hand. And there was the replica of my dog Watson, anatomically correct. And there were the wonderful abstract creations, as silky smooth and elegantly polished and sensually suggestive as any Henry Moore sculpture. Chunks of wood that guided you into their hearts and showed you their secret hidden forms. You were an artist, Dad. As complicated in your tastes and as sophisticated in your technique as any artist I know.

I have no children, so I can only guess at how difficult it must be to let them go, let them follow their bliss, especially when the bliss they follow conflicts so dramatically with your own better judgment. But I can say this, Dad. Were it not for your willingness to let me blunder ahead, or your endless encouragement, your silent support, your constant faith, I would not have become the man I am. You let me live for that summer in Greenwich Village when I was only nineteen and wanted to be a poet, an occupation that must have seemed to you the sheerest lunacy. "Are you sure this is what you want?" you would ask when I made some outlandish request. And if after deliberation I said yes, then yes was your most natural reply. When I asked you to write a letter to the local draft board in support of my application for conscientious objector status during the Vietnam War, you, a military school graduate and a major in the Army Reserves, wrote a letter that was both straightforward and eloquently moving, a letter that probably cost you enormous pain and embarrassment before the conservative townsfolk who made up that board. But you did it, and you did it beautifully, as you managed to do most things.

For you were an elegant man. A man of precision and old-fashioned courtliness. I always wondered if that had anything to do with how you were named. It is a rare name. Your father's name, my brother's, and his son. *Noble*. Highborn, aristocratic, admirable, of gentle birth. You were all those things. A lucky boy who at eleven had the wonderful duty of driving your father's drugstore delivery truck, an Austin, around the rutted muddy roads of western Kentucky with your dog Rex balanced precariously on the roof. There is a photograph of you at that age standing in front of the Austin and next to a girl, the girl who prompted you to sneak out of your boyhood upstairs window on many nights so you could talk to her, the girl who became my mother. She was taller than you then, looking straight into the camera, pretty and clear-eyed. And you looked noble even then. A small smile on your lips. The world opening before you, endless possibilities. A gracious boy, a smart boy who would learn to do a jackknife at the local ponds and would continue to do them well into middle age, a boy who would go to war and would stand on a snowy road and watch a fellow officer blown apart, a boy who loved to watch the dogwoods bloom and the pretty girls pass by.

Recently a banker described to me a study of the transfer of wealth that is now taking place between your generation, Daddy, and mine. I know you would be interested in what she told me because you too were a banker, and a good one, taking over the local savings and loan from your father, much as George Bailey did in *It's a Wonderful Life,* another man who made a quiet difference in so many people's lives. One fact this banker told me, Dad, is that the average time it takes a baby boomer like me to spend his entire inheritance is fourteen months. New cars, a vacation home, their kids' college education eat it up quickly. I know you would be dismayed yet unsurprised to consider that figure. Fourteen months. What took you and Mother a lifetime of thrift and attention and hard work to save gone in a fourteen-month splurge. Well, I want to let you know, Dad, that I'm going to beat the average on this one. I promise you that what I've inherited will last the rest of my days. I am determined to make it last, to husband each of the memories I've mentioned here and all the others that are just now beginning to resurface. I promise you, Dad, I won't squander the smallest bit of what you worked so hard to pass on.

I'm proud of you, Daddy, so proud. Of how you lived and how you died. Your courage, your stamina, your droll humor, your generosity to friends and acquaintances, your deep and abiding love for Mother. Like so many of my men friends, I longed for your approval and sanction, your blessing. And you were generous enough and wise enough to make sure I knew it was freely and truly given. Although in our last hours together, I tried to let you know some of the things I've mentioned in this letter, how much I respected and honored you, I needed to write it out, to shape the sentences, to make it flow from start to finish. This is another thing I learned from you, Daddy-O, whose well-shaped, gentle-spirited life will stand before me always, pointing the way.

Your son,

Jim

A MOVING EXPERIENCE

Psychologists who study traumatic life experiences consistently rank changing residences alongside severe illness, loss of loved one, divorce, and jail time. Well, this amateur psychologist who just spent the last couple of months engaged in the moving process would gladly have served the equal amount of time in a prison cell. At least there I might have been able to get a little writing done.

It started with the decision to sell our house. Although we'd dearly loved that charming wood cottage on an acre and a half, we had discovered that keeping the structure in good repair and the trees trimmed and the pool cleaned and the various pumps and motors running smoothly consumed a vast amount of our free time, not to mention an ever-increasing portion of our expendable income. Much to my dismay, I was on a first-name basis with the small army of experts it required to keep that wonderful old house from turning into a dilapidated shack.

We agreed, it was time for a simpler life. Time to

find a house with hurricane shutters that I could close in a few hours rather than the two days it took to lug sheets of plywood out of the shed and nail them into place. Two days to put them up, two days to take them down, a week before my backache went away. The more we thought about it, the more sense it made. We looked at our yearly expenses for maintenance, and the numbers were astonishing. There were big jobs looming on the horizon. Now was the time. The real estate market looked good. We could probably sell it fairly easily.

We sold it in two days. The sign went up, the offer came in.

And suddenly I was walking around our house of eight years, confronting the accumulated mass of our possessions. After a brief look in the attic, in storage cabinets, in the shed, my heart sank. In those eight years, my wife and I had managed to squirrel away enough books and dishes and files and Christmas decorations and more books and more files and more dishes to supply the needs of a midsize third world country. An embarrassment of excess.

Thus began the first phase of the move—purging. We had a garage sale and managed to unload five tons of worthless items. Junk we thought people would scoff at sold in the first hour. A ram's head that was losing its fur in handfuls, a dozen different nut dishes and cheese plates and rusty tools and broken fishing rods. We closed down the garage sale a couple of hours before noon, totally depleted. Then, in the flush of our triumph, we took a more careful look around our house, and to our horror we discovered that we'd overlooked a couple of truckloads of other useless items. Things we hadn't used or seen in years were gathering dust on some back shelf of the kitchen or pantry or broom closet.

I began making trip after trip to Goodwill. Then trip after trip to the dump. It was wonderful to cleanse away all that trash, get our life down to the essentials. No more conspicuous consuming for us. I kept thinking of Gandhi, who died with only a loincloth, a pair of sandals, and bifocals to his name. A saintly self-satisfaction fell over me. We were trimming our lives down to the basics.

Then we started to pack those essentials. Boxes and more boxes and more and more and more boxes began to clutter our house. The liquor store couldn't keep up with me. The U-Haul box salesman learned our names. Boxes filled with books. Boxes filled with plates and glasses and the ten thousand little geegaws we couldn't part with. Boxes and boxes. More and more boxes. And a wearying series of decisions. Will we ever use this? Will we regret tossing it away? Should I keep this or that because of the fairy dust of sentimentality attached to it?

Finally it was done. Everything was packed, but we were not even halfway to our goal. The date of the real estate closing was hurtling toward us. That's when we made our fateful decision and called the first name on our list of movers. I wish the laws of litigation were such that I could freely mention the name of the company. I would enjoy executing even a mild bit of revenge on this outfit for the wrenching anguish they put me through. But alas, a generic name will have to do. Let's call them Huey, Dewey, and Louie Scam-Artist Movers.

At the appointed hour two weeks before the move, Huey, Dewey, and Louie Scam-Artist Movers sent out their official estimator to look over our mountain of boxes and our furniture and our odds and ends. The estimator spent an hour with his legal pad walking from room to room, taking notes, making complex computations. Our hearts beat wildly. Could we even afford to pay for moving our appalling mass of possessions? Or would I once again have to enlist the cadre of friends and graduate students who had always moved me in the past? Surely the cost of Advil and Budweiser for that aching bunch of middle-agers would be less than the figure that this man with his yellow legal pad was coming up with.

When he presented his total, we were thrilled. It was manageable. A lot less than either of us had imagined. Without even calling for more estimates, we gave him a deposit and picked the date. He assured us that we would get the best team of movers he had. Huey, Dewey, and Louie themselves.

If there is a more hectic, stressful period of time than the days before and after a move, I have not discovered it. Keeping track of reading glasses and checkbooks and other essential paperwork as you unplug the last phone, empty out the last drawer, wade through the chaos of boxes is next to impossible.

The day arrives. The lawyers pass the unreadable papers around the desk, and the tectonic plates of our lives forever shift. We are on our way to somewhere else, a new beginning. Our blood pressure is soaring.

There is total disarray everywhere we look. And the movers are late.

This is part of the scam. This is an utterly premeditated decision. I can envision the scene. They have finished their morning move and are on their way to my house. It is one o'clock, the time they are scheduled to arrive. Huey turns to Louie and says, "Hey, whadda ya doing? You trying to be on time or what?" "Yeah, right," Louie says. "Let's stop for a two-hour lunch."

So they are late. And there are not many numbers left on my blood pressure gauge. I no longer own the house where all my earthly possessions sit. Boxes are clogging the doorways of a stranger's house. The minutes creep by. The hours mount. They are late. Later than late.

I call the company. "They're on their way. You're getting the first team. Huey, Dewey, and Louie themselves."

Finally they arrive. Their truck is smaller than I imagined. Not even big enough to haul our books. But I'm so relieved to see them, so overjoyed they have come to save me that I am ready to fall to my knees before them. Thank you, Huey.

But Huey says a quick hello and starts a fast circuit through the house. Something is wrong. He's frowning. He's grimacing. He's muttering. Something is very wrong. I think fondly of the prison cell. I fantasize about being in the hospital with a deadly disease. Anything would be better than this.

In two minutes he returns.

"What's wrong?"

"We can't do it."

"Can't do what?"

"They gave you a flat rate. But you got too much stuff. I can't move you for that amount."

"But I have a written estimate. I have it right here with all my other important documents. My birth certificate. My marriage license. My will."

He calls the boss and mutters to him for several minutes. I can't hear what he says. Then he hands me the phone. I'm in a dither. A mad panic. My stuff is sitting inside someone else's house.

The boss echoes what the driver has said. Their estimator was wrong. He was new. He got it all wrong. It was going to cost double.

"Double!"

"That's right. Double."

"I have a written estimate."

"We can't do it for that price," the boss says. "Either you pay double or call another mover."

It's now four o'clock. I haven't owned the house for three hours. They know all this. Huey, Dewey, and Louie do this all day. This is the scam. Lowball the estimate, then send in the driver with the shocked look and double the number.

"Okay, okay," I say. Thirty seconds into this, I'm caving in. I have no backup plan. There is no other mover standing in the wings ready to rush out and save me.

They begin to move my stuff. And it quickly becomes obvious that Huey, Dewey, and Louie don't like each other and they don't particularly like the moving business. They complain. They complain about my stuff. They complain about the boxes of books. They complain about the size of my couch. Then, when they hear that my new house has a second floor, they begin to complain about having to climb all those stairs.

At midnight it is clear that our stuff will not fit in their truck. Their truck is just the right size. It is my possessions that are out of whack. I'm to blame. They'll have to make two trips. This is going to cost hundreds more.

This time when they hand me the phone and the boss comes on to extort another few hundred dollars, I let go of a banshee rush of expletives. I tell him that he's a crook, that he's already scammed me out of a huge sum, and I simply won't pay another nickel. This is his problem. If he sent a truck that was too small, then that was his mistake.

"Give me back to Huey," he says.

Huey talks to the boss and hangs up. The several hundred extra bucks have disappeared. I'm thinking now that this racket depends completely on those trauma psychologists' ranking list. The moving company knows that this is one of the most stressful days of any person's life. They're like those vultures who swooped in after Hurricane Andrew to gouge us for roofs and ice. We were so worn down, so traumatized, we gave in without a fight.

So they moved me into my new house. My simpler life. They complained all the way. They left a pungent dose of bad karma in the air. But I left the windows open for a couple of days, and it has all blown away.

So now the real fun begins. Opening all those boxes. All those extra dishes and Tupperware bowls and beer steins I should have thrown away weeks ago.

Stuffing them into the back corners of the closets where they will sit until it is time for Huey, Dewey, and Louie to return. But next time I'll be ready. In my loincloth and sandals and bifocals, with my lawyer by my side.

CABO

Novels that tell a rousing good yarn while also containing a high dose of factual information about some esoteric subject matter have always been my favorite type of book. So from the beginning of my career, that's the kind I've tried to write.

Consequently, over the last thirteen years I've devoted about a month a year to researching my novels. Before I actually begin to write, I spend those four weeks reading in my chosen field and traveling to some place or another that I think will figure into the book somehow. For one book I journeyed to the jungles of Borneo to study orangutans, and a few years later I spent several difficult days as an observer in a pain clinic watching some rather exotic and excruciating medical procedures, so I could have sufficient realistic detail for another book. I've also gone deep into the stark, mosquito-infested interior of the state to observe the operations of fish farms, and I've stalked around some equally prickly parts of the Everglades to study the tricks of the trade used by animal poachers.

Since a good deal of the rest of my year is spent in virtual hibernation, I always look forward to this month of quasi-journalistic exploration. I interview people. I take lots of notes and shoot stacks of photographs. It's a time for soaking up material, for doing a quick study of my chosen subject, a month of total immersion that must provide me with enough authenticity and realism for the next eleven months of writing.

Although I think of myself as a moderately intelligent person, for some inconceivable reason I have chosen ten research projects in succession that required me to go to places I would never have chosen to visit otherwise. Not one vacation spot among them, not one five-star hotel or exotic port of call. Why, you might ask, did it never occur to me that I could just as easily write about locales I actually aspired to visit? How hard would it be to come up with a subject that absolutely required me to go to the Virgin Islands or Bimini?

Well, I'm happy to report that once I realized my error, it was not all that hard to correct. A while ago I decided that the research element for my next novel would concern big-time blue marlin fishing. I happened to know a couple of people who were intimately involved in the sport, and it sounded fascinating. And lo and behold, blue marlin fishing takes places in some pretty spectacular locales, places I've always wanted to visit. Cabo San Lucas, for one.

Because I picked my subject late in the fall, I had already missed the biggest and most famous blue marlin tournament, which also takes place in Cabo San Lucas. Bisbee's Black & Blue offers over two million dollars in prize money and costs several thousand to enter. Many of the best marlin fishermen in the world descend on Cabo during October to troll their lures through those marlin-rich seas. Though I'd missed the big one, there was one final tournament of the year that would fit my schedule perfectly. It was a modest one, with prize money in the six figures. It was run in part by the folks who publish *Marlin Magazine*. Though I knew no one at the magazine, when I contacted them by phone they assured me that if I wanted to get my journalistic feet wet in the world of big-time marlin fishing, I wouldn't be disappointed by their tournament. And they were certainly right.

Cabo San Lucas is the southernmost spot on the Baja peninsula. It roughly mirrors Key West's geographical position, a town at the end of the road dangling off the last spit of land on the opposite coast of America. Walk out of your hotel room, face the harbor, and the Pacific Ocean is on your right and the Sea of Cortez is on your left. The landscape is arid and dotted with sparse vegetation and a sprinkling of palms, and the mountains are jagged incisors, mostly barren outcroppings with a volcanic aspect. The town of Cabo San Lucas is planted on the side of one of those steep mountains, which plunges almost straight down a thousand feet below the surface of the sea.

There are no shallows in Cabo. A few yards off the sandy beach the water changes color abruptly to the deep blue of unfathomable depths. Talk about rip currents. The tidal flow caused by those deep drop-offs whisks around the tip of Baja and up into the Sea of Cortez at such a pace that swimming is not permitted off the beaches. A good place to hitch a ride to oblivion.

This was not to be a fishing trip. I came to observe the place and the people and the activities on land. I came to interview some people and meet others for future trips. I've fished for marlin before and plan on doing it again, but on this trip I was focused on the operation of the tournament itself. The good people from *Marlin Magazine* invited me along on the committee boat one dawn to watch the start of the day's fishing. Each of the boats must check in with the committee boat, passing close by and holding up its designated number, then taking its place behind an imaginary line drawn across the harbor. This was my chance to catch a quick glimpse of each boat and crew, and the range was strikingly diverse. From the sleek white seventy-footers that cost in the two- to three-million-dollar range, outfitted with the latest space-age electronics, glittering outriggers, huge gold reels, and neatly uniformed crew, to some local thirty-foot wooden vessels, grubby and hard-used, manned by ragtag troops who looked as if they might've been recruited at the last second from the gang of dockside waifs who sell counterfeit watches out of briefcases.

During the three days I was there, I interviewed people, took notes, shot photos, the usual stuff. But it wasn't until the last day that I felt the moment of revelation occur, that spike in my pulse that I'm always waiting for. It was the final evening of the tournament, and I was waiting at the dock with the growing crowd, some anglers who'd already returned and other tourists and locals who added to the buzz of excitement. By radio we'd learned that one boat was bringing back a big blue to be weighed on the official scales. While the tournament strongly encouraged a catch and release policy, now and then a fish was killed, either inadvertently or at the wish of the angler.

It was nearly eight o'clock when the big yacht backed up to the dock. The young, sunburned men unceremoniously hauled the fish through the stern door, flopped it on the concrete pier, and dragged it over to the rope and pulley system that was hooked to a scale. In the ghastly shine of the hotel spotlights, they cranked the big fish up by its tail. The crowd pushed close. It wasn't a monster, not even close to a record, but it was about twenty times bigger than any fish I've ever caught, and its blue sheen and its dead glossy eyes and its mangled spear brought a hush to the group. It was a sickening sight. It was a marvelous sight. This creature that cannot survive in captivity, that lives a life as elusive and unknown as practically any creature on the planet, this animal that fights with such picturesque displays of power and strength, tail walking on the ocean's surface, heart-stopping arabesques, reel-sizzling runs, this creature hung before us, grotesque and beautiful, beaten yet valiant.

The men who caught it were joyous. There were whispers in the crowd, subdued, almost funereal murmurs that sounded much like those on afternoons many years ago when I witnessed equally powerful and equally doomed bulls killed in the rings of Spain. A tragic spectacle. A ritual of solemn beauty.

I had come all that way to soak up a place, drink some Mexican beer, chat with some experts in the

field. And then I was blindsided by this. This powerful, irreconcilable contradiction. What more could I
have wished for? Though I'd picked the subject for all
the wrong reasons, at that moment I saw with stunning clarity that I'd chosen a subject that would challenge me to the core.

A WALK ON THE BEACH

No place in Florida is more than seventy miles from the beach. Ours is a state whose image is so dominated by the sandy strip along the water's edge that it is nearly impossible to think of Florida without picturing the lapping surf, the stalky birds, the daily dose of seashells washing ashore. In large measure it is the beach that draws the majority of our tourists. Even if they start at Disney World or Universal Studios, sooner or later most of them will head for the shoreline. The sugary Gulf beaches of Saint Pete and Siesta Key and Naples. The dunes and sea oats and unblemished stretches of the Panhandle. The wide white avenues of Daytona and Jacksonville. We are literally surrounded by that thin belt of sparkling grit, that fine sprinkle of pulverized crystal. It is to that place that we flock in large numbers to spread our towels, set up our lounge chairs, and soak up the soothing rays. It is our playground, our walking place, our sunset meditational spot. It is a place of romance and wildness where we go to seek out solace and rejuvenation.

Needing a little of both of those, my wife and I decided to go for a stroll on the closest beach. What we had in mind was a romantic moonlit ramble, something to loosen the knots in our corpuscles, freshen the oxygen supply in our blood. We chose a weeknight, early in the week, judiciously waited till after rush hour had died out, and headed for the seashore.

Thirty minutes later we were circling block after block searching for a place to park, our need for solace and rejuvenation growing with every revolution. There were dozens of valet-pilfered spots reserved for customers of the trendy restaurants. Row after maddening row of vacant parking spaces, their meters hooded with these private businesses' logos. Since we had not come for food, we passed by the valet parking, searching side streets and alleys up and down the entire strip of beach but finding nothing. Finally we located a miraculous opening three blocks from the ocean, squeezed into it, and poured quarters into the meter for several minutes.

A little frazzled but happy to be finally on foot, we ambled across the first thoroughfare in the pedestrian crosswalk and were almost run down by a guy in his top-down convertible. He was yammering away on his cell phone and clearly considered traffic laws less important than his conversation. As he whizzed by only inches away, I called out to him, registering my dismay, and he turned his head and screamed back at me, calling me a string of unprintable names.

We were within sniffing distance of the tangy seashore, already buffeted by gusts off the ocean, but we were feeling anything but relaxed. In one sense it seemed a wonderfully ironic south Florida moment—

that brief encounter with an inconsiderate driver as we headed for a tranquil walk on the beach. On the other hand, it cast a threatening pall over the moment. So much anger, erupting so easily between two apparently carefree citizens.

But we plowed ahead, determined to make the best of the evening, though both of us were wondering if the hothead in the convertible was at that moment circling back to stalk us along the beach. We took off our shoes, carried them along, crossed the small rise off the ocean boulevard, and there it was, spread before us in all its enduring and unruly majesty.

The water was green in the twilight, a lime color that seemed magical and unreal. There were few walkers, few joggers, only a huddle of homeless men sharing a bottle and some hardy laughs. We walked down to the edge of the Atlantic and cooled our feet in its foamy surf. We stood for a moment and took a lungful of that freshened air, gazing out at the ships heading into port. It was a moment that begged for platitudes about the wildness of the sea, its beauty and its danger. But we said little, just stood there ankle-deep in the surf and let the ocean work its fingers through our hair, massage those tightened muscles, ease the tension in our chests.

At that moment I remembered meeting a young man some years ago on a rafting trip in North Carolina. Coincidentally, he was from south Florida as well. He worked with at-risk kids, *delinquents* as we used to name them. One striking thing he said that day was that many of the kids he dealt with had lived in south Florida all their lives and had never even been to the beach. They knew every square inch of their neighborhoods, maybe a ten-square-block area, but they had no sense of the larger world. To provide them with that larger perspective, the program this gentleman worked with took groups of kids to live in isolated island environments. They lived on the beach. They spent their days on or in the water and spent their nights gazing out at more water. He claimed that the success rate of his program was something like ninety percent.

As we stood there watching the light fail, watching the ominous clouds gathering overhead, the endless drama of weather swirling all around us, feeling small yet vital, I could fully understand how such a program could succeed. The power of the beach, that juncture of land and sea, civilization and wilderness, order and disorder, is so resonant, so irresistible that it has an almost redemptive effect. Simply being there, standing in the face of that wind, looking out to sea, feeling that surge of primal sensations was enough to wash away the day's aggravations and indignities. Enough to grant forgiveness to the lout in his convertible, enough to remind us what luck we enjoy living in this place. Yes, yes, back across Ocean Drive, the stereos blare and the neon throbs and the cars cruise endlessly up and down in search of some nameless empty pleasure. But a few hundred yards away, the ocean thrashes against the sand and the air is filled with the wild, exotic scents of faraway lands, and we hold hands and we kiss, and though there is no moon, it is the romantic moment we were seeking. All is well. All is well.

Now for the trek back to our car.

DOGGONE

The first one was named Skippy. He was a Heinz 57 with a lot of terrier mixed into the sauce. Short-haired, black-and-white, and capable of countless cute poses in all those old snapshots in the family album. There's one where both of us are sprawled on our stomachs side by side on the living room rug, and he's pressing his nose to the corner of the page of the comic book I'm reading. Beyond those photos, though, I have no memory of Skippy. But surely, because there was a dog in my life at the ages of four and five, the groundwork was laid for a lifetime connection with the varmints.

Baby was the first dog I remember clearly. She was awarded that name because of the endless supply of puppies that flowed from her. She was a neighborhood dog, fed by everyone on our street, tolerated by everyone, though she spent more time in my yard than anywhere else. She was a mutt, white with yellow ears and a Lab's square face. She wagged her tail in a circle, which was only one signal of her general ungainliness. I remember her chasing rabbits in our yard, and more than once the rabbit veered left, and old Babe kept on heading straight and smacked right into the trunk of a tree. Wile E. Coyote and the Road Runner, beep beep.

I don't remember how she died. Disappeared, most likely. But I remember the deaths of other childhood dogs. There was Richie, named after a TV detective at the time, Richard Diamond. Richie had a diamond-shaped white mark on his throat, which gave him a rakish quality. He was another wild mix of breeds, larger than a terrier but smaller than a Lab. He liked to chase cars. Actually, he liked to chase the front right tires of cars, snapping and yapping just inches from the whirling rubber, sprinting along the shoulder of the road till the car gained enough speed and moved out of his territory. It was daredevil work. And though I carried out the official doctrine of our family and tried to discourage Richie from chasing, I secretly considered it a noble sport. Outmatched in size and speed, Richie never grew weary of the game. Not every car drew his interest, but those that did brought out speed and aggression that were truly breathtaking to behold.

Of course a car hit him finally. We heard him squealing and came running. He'd already dragged himself into a culvert and crawled deep inside a drainage pipe. He was still alive. We could see him cowering in there. Since I was the smallest, it fell to me to climb inside that damp space and haul him out. He snapped at me, but I knew that unless we got him out of there he would die for sure, so I managed to grab the scruff of his neck and drag him out, taking several nicks in the process. Later the next day it was obvious Richie was broken in too many places to survive, and my dad took him out into the far reaches of the property and shot him with a rifle. The whole family wept.

I still can hear the single crack of that rifle shot.

I think of it each time I've had to put one of our dogs to sleep. With Watson, a Saint Bernard–Labrador mix, it eventually became clear that he could no longer pull himself up off the rug. His hips had given out. I called the vet, made the fateful appointment, then on the way there we stopped at a 7-Eleven and bought Watson his favorite beverage, a cold Budweiser. On the surgical table, he lapped up that beer, gave us all a happy grin, then the vet administered the shot. Though nothing can alleviate the grief that comes at such moments, we always repeat the mantra "He had a great life. He was the luckiest dog there was. All the rawhide chewies, all the pig ears, all the Frisbees he could consume. He was a great dog."

And when sufficient healing time has passed, there is the inevitable puppy. The ride home with the new pup is always joyous, but somehow tinged with the tragedy to come. We know we will see them die. It flavors every moment of their life in some quiet way. But still we cannot help ourselves. Though the pain of their loss is great, the loss of their joy-giving would be even more difficult. So there is another puppy. Another mutt to train, to housebreak, to test our consistency and discipline. Another puppy that will use any trick to subvert our iron wills. Face-licking works nicely, or clumsy cavorting, and sleeping on their back with all four paws in the air will do the job quite well.

Puppies make suckers of us all. We cannot resist. We'll let them in the bed, let them prop their head on our pillow. We let them lick our plates, we let them chew our fingers to bloody pulp, and we let them climb onto the couch and curl up and snore. We do all this knowing full well we'll regret it later. We vow to be tougher next time. The next dog will be absolutely and utterly under our control. But alas, that never happens. And we wouldn't want it to, not really. We don't want our dog to chase cars or to bark incessantly or pose a threat to the mailman. But now and then we want it to erupt into effervescent displays of wildness. To run amok in its fenced yard, to let loose with a howl of pleasure, a yippee, a hoot. To chase a butterfly until it's dizzy.

Our floors are tracked with paw prints. Tumbleweeds of fur grow in the corners. The rug gradually changes its color to the shade of their coats. We live with their sweet, suffocating, haylike aroma. Their hair is on our sweaters, our sport coats, on clothes we haven't even bought yet. Our sleep patterns are altered by the groans and twitches of their rabbit-chasing dreams. We cannot take spur-of-the-minute trips anymore but must find a dog-sitter as indulgent and neurotically absorbed in their welfare as we are. They are the children we never had. They are our perpetual two-year-olds.

We watch them sleep. We watch them stare at the squirrels. We watch them watching us. There are a thousand smiles that we would never have enjoyed without these dogs. A thousand chuckles, a thousand outright guffaws, a thousand heartaches. These puppies who grow large and grow old and can no longer pull themselves up off the floor. We need them as desperately as they need us.

ANNIVERSARY

It's been almost a year since my father died. Though the intensity of pain at losing him has subsided an iota, his passing still figures into almost every decision I make these days, every action I take, large or small. Everything from deciding to sell one house and move to another, to making small refinements in my diet. I find myself continually taking fresh looks at my habits and manner of spending time. Everything seems up for inspection and review.

Just after his death a year ago, I thought it would be simple from that moment on to sustain a carpe diem state of mind. My father made it very clear that this was his wish for me. During a phone conversation in his final year, I mentioned that I'd just that afternoon broken a tooth. His reaction was swift and flabbergasting.

"Take all the trips you're going to take. Go all the places you want to go. This is how it starts."

"How what starts?"

"The end of your life."

"With a broken tooth!"

"Don't wait to do the things you've been dreaming of."

"Okay, okay."

But the carpe diem way of life is easier to imagine than to carry out. For me the daily wrestling match between the need for security and the desire to take risks tilts inevitably toward the side of security. Maybe not so fundamentally as it did in my parents' post-Depression mentality, but it tilts that way just the same. So how is it possible to seize the day without taking risks? Isn't the natural antagonist of an adventuring spirit that small, insistent voice of reason that whispers its worries in our inner ear? *Are you sure you want to take that trek into the Alaska wilderness? Wouldn't that money be better spent on investments to ensure a more secure old age?* I struggle with this, as I know my father did. I want to ask him for clarification. But of course he is no longer there.

In this last year at least a dozen of my friends have also lost parents. We have been suffering the cycle together. The terrible diagnosis, the excruciating treatments, the slow decline, the occasional rallies and remissions, and inevitably the final moment. We try to share what insights we've managed to gain from our own parents' deaths. But it's not always easy.

When one of my close friends' mother was diagnosed with liver cancer, she chose to forgo chemotherapy, deciding instead that she would die in her own home, surrounded by her possessions, her thousand happy memories. Having witnessed the endless invasions of privacy and the sterile, noisy atmosphere of the hospital where my father spent his last months, I celebrated her decision. But was it any better to die at home under hospice care? My friend who witnessed his mother's last days reported that there came a point fairly early on when the prized possessions and familiar surroundings meant nothing anymore. Dying was dying. The slow unraveling of the body and spirit was just as painful to experience and just as heart-wrenching to behold wherever it took place.

Because I am a writer, I find that much of my thinking is shaped by the structural paradigm of the three-act play or novel. For me the life story and the archetypal dramatic story merge. Act One is clearly about youth. The setting of goals, the shaping influences, a spurt of growth that culminates in some galvanizing moment that sends the hero off on his quest.

As the curtain comes down on Act One, our hero is crossing the threshold, on his way out of the safety and protection of the only home he's known, the walled city. He is marching away into the great unknown. Which means, of course, that Act Two is all about his struggles to accomplish his goals, seize the holy grail. Small-town boy goes to the big city, rising above its corrupting influence. Complications abound. The going is rough, but he forges on, ever resourceful, surmounting each new hurdle thrown before him, until finally some stunning reversal occurs. His quest is radically altered by an unexpected yet perfectly predictable event. His father dies. His world is shaken to the core. The curtain lowers, and the curtain immediately rises.

Now it is Act Three. The time for resolutions. Tying up all the loose ends. The final third of this drama is the time when the wisdom collected on the journey so far must begin to pay off. If peace can be achieved, this is the last stretch of time to find it. If there is to be joy or understanding or enlightenment, then they must come very soon.

That's where we are, my friends and I. We have lost our parents and the homes where we grew up. We are exiles now, for there is no longer a walled city to return to. The homes we have managed to create for ourselves are from this moment on the only homes we have. Our one abiding safe haven has vanished forever.

We have also lost our wise counsel, our protector, our buffer against death. Our end looms out in the distant, uncertain future. The curtain trembles overhead. We must face this last third with whatever resources we have mustered on our journey: intelligence, faith, resilience, love, friendship.

Seizing the day seems to play only a minimal role in my version of this final act. Of course, I've vowed to accomplish some of my father's unfulfilled dreams. I'm going to travel more. I'm going to visit some of those places he always wanted to see. And I'm going to take him along with me to other spots he never imagined.

But there are larger issues to resolve in this last act. More to do than simply indulge our senses on our parents' behalf. They fought wars and endured punishing hardships so that we might know freedom. They were decent people who sacrificed their own economic well-being to leave us a legacy of comfort and hope. We owe them more than simply a eulogy and a self-gratifying carpe diem approach to life. We need to strive for the nobility all heroes seek in the final act. The curtain has gone up. One third of the play is left, a final chance to transform ourselves into individuals worthy of the parents we have lost.

FAITHLESS IN SOUTH FLORIDA

I have been unfaithful. I have spent precious time with another, betraying all that I cherish. I have strayed far from home, indulging myself in the fresh scents and fascinating newness, the sweet undulations of virgin terrain and the wild, reckless abandon of exploring new delights. With relish and jubilation, I have wallowed in iniquity all through the gorgeous and aromatic nights, then leaped up at dawn to make merry all the following day.

Yes, it is true. I am most grievously ashamed to admit that I have spent the summer in the mountains of North Carolina, and I liked it. I liked it a lot.

For thirty years I have been loyal to summertime in Florida. Indeed, I have joined with others in the mythmaking that we depend on to survive the intense torment of a subtropical June, July, August, and September. For one thing, we like to tell ourselves that by enduring the gruesome heat and humidity, we have enriched our character, paid our moral dues, so that we can more deeply appreciate those silky January days when they finally arrive.

Well, fie on that. I've paid my dues already, thanks. Thirty summers in Florida ought to earn me sufficient frequent perspiration miles to ride free from here on out. And anyway, I have begun to harbor serious doubts about the karmic payoff for self-inflicted suffering. What merit badges have we earned by braving melanoma and heatstroke or, more likely, by sitting indoors twenty-four hours a day in the expensive machine-driven air of our homes and cars and offices?

Another myth we like to trot out each June is that it is just as hot or hotter elsewhere around the contiguous forty-eight as it is in south Florida. Baltimore in August, New York City, New Orleans, certainly they're more insufferable than Miami. After all, as the myth goes, we have those lovely sea breezes shaving off five or six degrees from the ninety-sevens and ninety-eights we see on the weather map elsewhere.

Well, if you believed that, you'd be wrong. Baltimore, New York, and New Orleans all have lower average temperatures in August than Miami. Because when you're discussing temperature, what matters is not just how hot it gets, but also how cool. The only spot in America that I could locate with a hotter average temperature than south Florida is Death Valley, California. So, for those die-hard believers in the virtues of broiling human flesh, may I suggest the Death Valley Motel 6 for your next summer destination?

And finally there is the South Florida Chamber of Commerce propaganda, which would have us believe that to desert our lovely paradise during the summer months is to miss the best fishing, boating, outdoor season of the year. The lobsters, the dolphin, the bonefish, all stupefied from the overheated water, are supposedly easy prey. The ocean is never more inviting, the summer rates are down from their stratospheric highs, lots of bargains everywhere. See Florida, explore your own backyard. Stay home and sweat. And swat.

About the only good argument for Florida summers I can manage is that the roads are slightly less terrifying in August than in January. With all the Canadians and New Yorkers and Germans back home in their chalets, there is probably a slightly better chance of avoiding a fatal eruption of road rage.

Obviously a good many other south Floridians have also abandoned these stay-at-home myths, because the back roads of North Carolina are filled with Dade and Broward and Palm Beach license plates. Miraculously, most of my fellow Floridiots (as some Carolinians refer to us) seem to tame their aggressive tendencies and actually fall into the same mellow biorhythms as the mountain folks. For an entire month I didn't hear a single horn honk, nor did I witness any tailgating, lane-hopping, bird-flipping madness, those mainstays of our daily driving diet.

It's a kinder, gentler place, the North Carolina mountains. And cooler. Much, much cooler—some sixteen degrees on average than sunny south Florida. There was, in fact, one August morning when we woke with the bedroom windows wide open, and lo and behold we could see the fog of our breaths. I jumped out of bed, hurried downstairs to check the outside thermometer.

Forty-eight degrees.

There was only one sane reaction to such an event.

We built a fire. After all, in south Florida on a cool January morning, say fifty-five degrees or so, we bundle up in our sweaters, tear open the plastic bag of split cherry, toss in the kerosene-soaked starter log, and light up the fireplace. Fifty-five degrees is all it takes to set these events in motion, so at forty-eight it was clearly obligatory.

Our neighbors, locals all, immediately went into a panic. They thought we'd set our house on fire. Several of them showed up in our driveway with extinguishers. And when I told them all was well, the fire was safely within the fireplace, only meant to chase the chill, they gave me that look that is reserved for errant children and the harmlessly deranged.

Forgive me, Florida, for I have sinned. I have been with another.

For three decades I have been devout in my loyalty to all things Floridian. And I have been an ardent believer in the aforementioned myths, which helped sustain me through thirty shirt-soaked summers. So this change of heart has come as a shock to me. I didn't realize how pleasant it could be to hike six miles along the Appalachian Trail and not be soaked with perspiration. I never fully appreciated the art or splendor of fly-fishing for trout in a cold and isolated river where it is highly likely that in a day's time you will see more fish than people. I had no idea what luxury it could be to sit outside on the back porch in the chill of an August evening and watch the darkness bloom with fireflies.

Forgive me, Florida, for I have strayed. I have let another into my heart.

CAMPING OUT

When I was nine years old my parents delivered my older brother and me to a summer camp in North Carolina. But this was not just any summer camp. This was the same camp my father and his brother had attended in their youth, the camp whose very cabins and lodges my father and uncle had helped construct from venerable pines and oaks. Going to camp was as close to a family tradition as we had. It was both my duty and my privilege to follow in my elders' footsteps and spend five glorious weeks at Camp Sequoyah.

That moment when my brother and I were first delivered to camp is forever blazed in my memory. Our old Rambler crunched up the gravel drive and passed beneath the wooden sign with Sequoyah carved deep into its grain. A stream gurgled beside the roadway. The cool shadows were scented with pine and the pleasant mildewy fragrance of old buildings newly opened.

We hauled out our duffel bags, met our counselors, bid our teary parents good-bye, and marched off into that wooded, secluded, mountaintop retreat. Thus began my first extended stay away from my parents' influence, my first encounter with a larger cross section of folks than I would ever have known existed had I stayed home to swim in the Kiwanis Pool and while away the summer playing sandlot basketball or roaming the farms of my school friends.

I never suffered from homesickness as so many of my fellow campers did. Camp struck me immediately as one long feast of opportunities. The chance to learn woodcraft skills and the secrets of compass and map reading. Discovering the names of constellations and birds and flowers and trees and wild edible fruits. Archery and rifle practice. Twilight battles of capture the flag. Five weeks of tying lanyards, playing tetherball, hiking the steep, slick trails of western North Carolina, camping overnight, listening to ghost stories that still to this day give me chills. And learning the dances and crafts and folklore of the Cherokee Indians who had once inhabited those very hills.

Indian lore it was called. We made our own loincloths and headdresses. We beaded moccasins and formed spears from birch saplings, we learned the Cherokee alphabet and a few of the strange, potent words of that tribe. A few hundred upper-middle-class boys from all over the South spent part of that five-week session pretending with great seriousness that we *were* Native Americans, stalking those ancient woods in our beaded leather slippers, speaking to each other in the magical grunts and vowel-laden phrases of the Cherokees.

By the time I was seventeen, I had outgrown the status of camper. Reluctantly I had graduated. The only way I could return to Sequoyah was to work there. Having observed firsthand how demanding and stressful a counselor's life could be, I chose another path. I became a kitchen employee, which meant that I spent four or five hours a day washing pots and scraping leftover food into the slop bucket that would later go to a local hog farmer. Along with a half dozen other teenage boys, I mopped floors and set tables and generally became a lackey for three hundred campers and their counselors.

The upside of this new position was that I could still swim in the lake, play tennis, hike, and participate in a great many of the organized activities of the camp, only now I was able to have my fun completely unsupervised. And miracle of miracles, I got paid for my pleasure. Some time during that summer I was struck with the realization that it was not only possible but absolutely crucial that I find a way to make my vocation my avocation. It was a watershed revelation. For my observations of the adult world until that moment had led me to believe that for most people work was work and play was play, and the two were never to be confused.

I felt like a sneak, a defector from the Work Ethic. I had found a way to have my cake and wallow in it too. For the next couple of summers I returned to Sequoyah in my new liberated status, and though I worked hard and long, it never seemed like work. I arrived at camp before the first campers and left after the last car had driven away. I swept away the cobwebs in June and put the final coat of wax on the floors in August. I stayed for both five-week sessions, longer than any counselor, longer than anyone except the owner of the camp himself.

For many years I believed I wanted his job. What could be better than to live in the big log cabin with my wife and spend every summer singing camp songs and presiding over the camp meetings? To be revered by generations of young men, to live in those magical hills all fall and winter and through the early spring, awaiting the new crop of disciples. I remember sharing my dreams with one of the venerable gentlemen who had made such a decision himself. He wasn't the owner of the camp, but he had been there every summer since the beginning. I forget his name or his title, but we considered him our resident wise man. He was a musician and a scholar, and even in his seventies he had a boyish twinkle in his eyes.

That day when I told him that I wanted a similar life to his, he smiled innocently, then got up from his chair, went into his bedroom, and came back with a slender volume.

"Read this," he said. "I think you'll like it."

That was all he said, no explanation, no further encouragement.

I took the book in my hand, looked at its title. It was one I had heard mentioned in my first year in college, but I had thought it too difficult to bother with. *A Portrait of the Artist as a Young Man*. I read it immediately and came back to talk about it with the wise old gentleman who had given it to me. But he wasn't interested in literary discussion. He just listened to me ramble on about the book, then shook his head and smiled.

I read it again, and this time I felt the full crushing weight of James Joyce's vision. Yes, it was possible and utterly necessary to fuse work with play. But I could not stay in the Eden of summer camp forever. As much as I loved that place, I had to leave, take my chances in the bigger world. I had to find some other way to escape the Work Ethic. I had to discover a higher order of play.

Today I can't smell a forest of pines or tramp up a steep mountain slope without instantly revisiting that place and time. I might have become the same person I am today without Camp Sequoyah. But I doubt it. I doubt it very much.

I'D LIKE TO THANK YOU ALL FOR COMING

I was in Saint Paul, Minnesota, a couple of winters ago. January, noon, downtown at a Barnes & Noble. It was a dreary twenty-four degrees, and there were some drizzles of snow mingled with the exhaust fumes and the razory wind. Another cheery moment on the glamorous book tour.

After wandering around for half an hour in the numbing cold searching for the bookstore, I finally found it and went inside. As soon as I defrosted, I located the special-events coordinator and introduced myself as the speaker for the day. She was a cordial young lady, and after a little chitchat about the weather (she thought it was a pretty nice day), she led me over to their reading corner, where there were twenty or so comfortable chairs spread around the small podium where I would make my edifying remarks, hoping to stimulate a frenzy of impulse buying of my latest novel.

Lo and behold, the chairs were filled. A noontime crowd of twenty or so people, a little scruffy-looking, perhaps, but fans nonetheless. My heart leaped up to think that somehow enthusiasm for my south Florida thrillers had penetrated to these icy climes. All these people had decided to take an hour out of their lives so that I could entertain them.

The special-events lady went back to her main desk and made an announcement over the store's PA system that the author James W. Hall had arrived and would shortly give a reading of his work in the west alcove.

Even as the echo of her voice was dying out, each and every person occupying the comfy chairs of the reading area stood up, pulled on his or her heavy coat, and filed toward the exit.

I was speechless. And audienceless.

When the special-events lady came back to join me, I asked what in the world had happened to my audience.

"Oh, they're street people," she said. "We let them come in out of the cold, but they know the drill. When an author shows up, they have to give up their seats."

Not only had I lost my crowd, but I had exiled a host of desperate souls back out to the frigid streets. Was anything I had to say worth that?

For the next hour I hung around and talked to my two legitimate Saint Paul fans and tried to keep from looking out the large windows, where the street people were milling around, slapping their arms, casting frequent looks into the store to see if the visiting writer had left yet.

Ah, yes. Just one more stop on the great ego-adjustment tour.

Only a few years earlier I would've traded a major organ for the chance to go out on a book tour. Traveling around the country to promote a book I'd written, meeting adoring fans, and being interviewed on television by savvy journalists had been a lifelong fantasy. How could such an experience be anything but glorious?

Later on that same day in Saint Paul, I was scheduled for a two-hour visit to the largest bookstore in the largest mall in America. The booksellers were thrilled I was there and were sure my fans would show up in droves. They had ordered sufficient books to provide the reading material for three European countries for a year. Hundreds of my books were stacked from floor to ceiling. They filled the window, they crowded out every other book in the store. A customer shopping for Grisham or Steele or Updike had to push aside a dozen James W. Halls to even get near their desired books.

I was fifteen minutes early and by then almost recovered from my morning's debacle. The mall was packed with people. Tour buses filled the parking lots, every escalator had a long waiting line. And I smelled disaster.

But on the book tour, disaster has many faces. On this particular afternoon, not a single fan of south Florida thrillers showed their face at the largest bookstore in the largest mall in America. They stayed away in droves. Great herds of people didn't show. There was no need for barricades. All the extra security guards were sent home. Nobody showed. Nobody. Zip. Two hours of aching humiliation, chatting with the booksellers, all of us putting on the bravest possible front. Not since my first book signing in a desolate mall in Daytona Beach, where my father showed up with his camera to take endless snapshots of me sitting alone at my signing table, had I felt such utter shame.

Finally, as I was about to leave, bidding farewell to my bosom buddies the booksellers, a middle-aged man came bounding up to me and breathlessly demanded to know if I was James W. Hall. Yes, I said. I was indeed.

"I'm so glad you haven't left. I've driven two hours to get here."

I beamed.

"Well, it's nice to meet you," I said. "So you're a fan of the books?"

"No," he said. "I haven't read any of them. But I had to have one."

"Oh, really," I said. Hearing the pitter-pattering steps of doom.

"Yeah, you know why?"

"Why?" I said.

"Because my name is James W. Hall, and I wanted to have a book with my name on it."

Ah, yes. Ah, yes.

That night in the hotel room I called my publicist, who had become my part-time therapist on that particular book tour. I told him I had a great new promotional idea. Before I arrived in any new city, he would call every James Hall in the phone book and ask, "Do you want a book with your own name on it?" I was sure to get a turnout that way. At least as good as I was getting.

There are lots more stories. Oh my, there are hundreds more. Some even better than these. Some so humiliating that I have to be put in deep hypnosis to recall the particulars.

Now, in fact, when I go out on a tour, as I must again very soon, I take along my pocket notebook so I don't forget a single nuance of each new mortification. As my therapist likes to say, you can never have too many self-deprecating anecdotes.

HURRICANES

This week its name was Floyd. It had a different history and a slightly different journey across the Atlantic, but for those of us who seven years ago were in the direct path of Hurricane Andrew, the scenario was hauntingly similar. In an instant all the terror and helplessness flooded back, the naked vulnerability, the breathless panic. Here was a storm as big as Texas, an angry swirl of wind and lightning, a tornado to the hundredth power. And it had us dead in its sights.

Seven years ago the weathermen assured us it would turn right. The brightly colored forecast track showed Hurricane Andrew brushing the south Florida coast, then making a northwest curve, steered by upper level highs or a dip in the jet stream. In the thirty years I had lived in Florida I'd never suffered a direct hit from a hurricane, but I boarded up as usual, and all evening we sat in the dark watching the weather on television as the big storm spun toward us like the ragged blade of a buzz saw. The forecasters seemed confident in their projections. Their wind charts and vapor loops and sophisticated computer models all suggested the same thing—we would get some strong gusts, a good dose of rain, then this big inconvenience would shift north to harass some less fortunate souls. So I went to bed that night sore from my labors and convinced that it was wasted effort, that the storm would follow their predictions, deflected by forces I barely understood.

But they were wrong. It didn't turn. Instead, around midnight, as Hurricane Andrew passed over the warm waters of the Gulf Stream just offshore of Miami, the storm strengthened to a category 4 with wind speeds approaching 150 miles an hour and continued on its previous heading.

The rising winds woke me. When I switched on the television, I went numb. Andrew had bulled past the steering currents and was heading directly for south Florida. In fact, the eye of the storm, around which the most furious winds circulate, was roaring toward the shoreline only a few miles from my home.

Before I could even register what I'd seen, there was an enormous crash outside. Peering around the plywood, I saw that the graceful Indian rosewood tree that shaded a large portion of the yard had been knocked flat. And Andrew had not yet come ashore.

At 3:15 A.M. the power went off. I remember the time so clearly because all the clocks in our house were frozen on that number for the next three and a half weeks until the electricity was finally turned back on. For the next three hours, in the utter darkness, we patrolled the house searching for any signs of damage. All around the neighborhood, electric transformers high up on telephone poles exploded and sent bursts of eerie blue light radiating around the edges of the plywood. The blasts of wind rose to such a pitch that it was no longer simply noise but a palpable vibration that rattled the marrow and made breathing an act of will.

In the midst of the tumult we heard a popping sound like muffled gunfire. Our shingles were flying off, one by one, the nails that held them down torn loose by the relentless wind. And then the water started coming in. Trickles at first. We put buckets under every leak until we'd used them all, as well as the pots and pans. Then we gave up on all but the largest gushes. The ceiling in the bedroom began to sag.

At one point, nearly overcome by the false fatigue of terror, I leaned against an interior wall but found that it was shuddering so hard I was bounced away. Underfoot the floor was shifting, and the deepening low pressure gave us a sinking sensation, as if the plane we were strapped into was in a fatal dive. Later I would find an exterior door that had been rattled so hard by the storm that the screws had worked loose, so that when I opened it, all the brass hardware fell to the ground. It had been hanging by a thread. The same thread that our lives had been suspended on without our knowing it. For a single breach was all it took to destroy a house.

That's what happened to my neighbors across the street. Their front door blew in, and the second story was flooded with wind, and the walls exploded. Luckily the husband and wife and three young children had already retreated to the ground floor—there are no basements here, no way to hide yourself below ground or root yourself to the earth. We found them the next morning, huddled in the downstairs bathroom with a mattress pressed to the door, knee-deep in water and completely unaware that their second story was gone.

We had all gone to bed the night before in modern America, and we stepped out the next morning into a wilderness that none of us had ever known. Houses destroyed, cars crushed, roads impassable. Our lush neighborhood devastated with hardly a tree standing. Not a leaf in sight. The mangoes gone, the wispy Australian pines crushed, the avocado trees broken in half. Fences vanished. No power lines anywhere, no street signs, no mailboxes. We were anonymous, stripped of our numbers, left to our own meager survival skills. A group of people who barely knew each other but who now were totally dependent on the talents of their neighbors.

There was the neighbor who had a neat system for siphoning gas to run the generators. The neighbor who could jury-rig the well pumps. The ones who were expert with a chain saw. Or could mix a good margarita. We propped each other up emotionally, giving what comfort we could in brutally raw moments of anguish and grief. In those next few grueling weeks, a dozen of us forged a bond as deep as any I've ever known. We are beyond friends. We are fellow survivors. Even seven years later, these are the people I most want to have as my neighbors in good weather and bad.

So this week, when Floyd began to gather strength, we shared a common sentiment. Call it pre–traumatic stress syndrome. Call it dread. But we made our jokes and went about our business, putting up the shutters, storing up supplies, far better prepared than last time in all the physical ways, but a great deal more vulnerable emotionally. Because we know the cycle. We know what awaits if this one comes ashore. The hours of terror as the walls begin to tremble and the trees break in half and all the unsecured debris for miles around becomes missiles. We know the aftermath. The long weeks of stupefying heat, the ceaseless snarl of generators and chain saws and helicopters flying overhead. We have seen our houses fill with ticks, which before the storm had been living harmlessly in the high branches of trees. We know what it is like to live for years without a bit of shade. To lust for ice and a hot shower.

Years ago I was in Los Angeles when a 6.2 earthquake hit the city. I raced down from my hotel room in a panic and joined the other guests who had assembled in the lobby. "Go back to your rooms," the manager instructed us. "It's all over now." How did he know that? Did he have a hot line to the tectonic plates? But we went back to our rooms, and indeed it was over except for some heavy-duty cleanup and bridge reconstruction. It was all so sudden—a disaster without an attention span. So appropriate for California, and so different from a hurricane with its slow and ominous buildup.

Hurricanes grow like good stories. They start out innocently with those deceptively simple rain showers off the African coast. But as they move past the Cape Verde Islands and into warmer waters, they begin to take a shape, a mild accumulation of power. When their pressure drops low enough and their spinning form finally becomes discernible, they are given a name. And it is this name we will know them by forever. Floyd, Gert, Andrew, Gloria, David, Opal, Hugo. When they have their names, we begin to pay attention. Our hairs prickle. We see them moving vaguely in our direction. We see the counterforces coming from the western half of the continent, forces that may or may not intersect with the approaching storm to nudge it this way or that.

It is a drama in which timing becomes everything. Will the jet stream trough dive deep enough? And will it do it in time? That is the nature of dread. The slowly gathering suspense, the tension-mounting worry. In that way these storms are strikingly different from tornadoes or earthquakes, which hit so quickly there is no time for much trepidation. Those disasters are mostly about the cruel and difficult aftermath. While hurricanes are large lumbering creatures that stalk their target with slow and indifferent menace. They build and grow. They tick forward in such slow increments that we have both the luxury and the curse of large amounts of time to get ready for their arrival. Is this a true change of course, or merely a wobble?

I shutter some windows and go inside to check Floyd's path. I go back to my windows and decide the shutters don't yet have enough screws tightening them down. How many is enough? Will that one missed corner of that one sheet of plywood be a lethal oversight?

For I know that hurricane winds can locate and exploit any weakness. I drill and drill, and Floyd ticks forward and ticks forward again.

This time they were right. The trough arrived in the final seconds, and Floyd veered mercifully to the northwest. I wonder why we don't give these saving troughs a name. But the deep relief I feel is fleeting. For our deliverance surely spells another's disaster. And because I know some of what awaits them, and what may yet await me this season or the next, I can find little comfort in my good fortune.

CHEETO

Okay, I admit it. In the last twenty-nine years, I have wasted literally thousands of glorious south Florida afternoons sitting indoors with my Cheetos and beer watching sports on television.

But in my defense, I have to say that I don't watch indiscriminately. I'm not some Lay-Z-Boy slob with an ice chest at my left hand and a bunch of pizza-eating bozo friends over to scream at the set. No, I'm a loner. And I'm a highly disciplined watcher of sports. With the one exception of the University of Kentucky basketball team, I only watch south Florida teams, or their future or past opponents. And though I shudder to admit it, I only watch on a regular basis when the south Florida team is having a winning year.

I know, I know. To the true sports fanatic, I'm a disgrace. Lower than pond scum. Yeah, yeah, yeah. But my position on this matter is simple. Why should I give up my glorious Saturday and Sunday afternoons to eat Cheetos in front of the television for a bunch of overpaid slobs who are losing?

I understand there's some kind of code among certain fans that unless you actually pack up your gear and go to the stadium or arena you aren't a true fan. And you lose points if you're a Johnny-come-lately, supporting the Panthers only when they've got a shot at the Stanley Cup or rooting for the Marlins only in their championship year. Well, fine. I'll gladly go to the back of the line when all the sports fans line up at heaven's gate. But I've got better things to do than root for guys who aren't going to let me bask in their reflected glory.

The one exception to this rule is the Dolphins. I landed in south Florida just a year after the perfect season when Shula was in the full flower of his glory. I watched every game and was imprinted deeply with that saintly glow Shula and all the Dolphins of that era radiated. Year after year the Dolphins were the least penalized team in football. We were gentlemen. We played fair. And we still managed to beat the ever-loving tar out of those dirty Oakland and Buffalo teams.

Out of some kind of addle-brained nostalgia, I still watch nearly every game even though Shula has been replaced by his Brylcream evil twin and the millionaire whiners of today couldn't carry the petrified jockstraps of Csonka and Kiick and Griese. I turn on the set even though I know that watching Jimmy Johnson work his much-vaunted psychology on his players today will make me cringe. The games Jimmy played with his team had about as much connection to psychology as the Spice Girls' singing had with music. Lucille Ball was more crafty. Lou Costello could finesse better.

As befits the current state of south Florida culture, we are no longer the least penalized team in the league. The current philosophy seems to be that if a fan wants to watch a bunch of polite, chivalrous, by-the-book athletes, they should order the ballroom dancing channel. Indeed, this new vision seems to have been spawned a few years back when that same Jimmy guided our most prominent college football team to national prominence as the bully boys of the gridiron. The Hurricanes of those national championship teams played a brand of in-your-face football that seemed perfectly suited to the south Florida reputation at the time. We were the town of cocaine cowboys and *Miami Vice*, outrageous acts of incivility that gave our town a kind of outlaw glamour.

South Florida seems to put its special stamp on all its sports teams. For instance, it seems disingenuous that there are those who cry foul when the Marlins trade away their World Series–winning team and replace them with inexpensive imitations. Why did we ever believe that a guy who made his fortune selling off his assets over and over would keep together a bunch of guys in aquamarine uniforms just because they'd won the World Series? What money builds, money tears asunder.

I admit I'm not a financial genius, but would someone explain to me how it's possible not to make money off a World Series–winning team? I suppose there are those who'd say it is actually my fault, because I'd rather not have to drive two hours so I can sit three hundred yards away from the field and sweat. Is my need for air-conditioning and Cheetos responsible for the downfall of major league baseball in south Florida? Probably.

Well, how 'bout those Panthers?

I had never watched an entire hockey game until two years ago, the year of the RAT. But I got swept up in the giddy hype to the point that I was actually willing to learn what the blue line was, and icing, and I went to the optometrist to increase my prescription so I could follow the puck. On two occasions I even joined with my neighbors and watched some of the games. We had a bucket of rats that we threw at the TV screen every time something the least bit interesting happened. It was fun. I was actually wasting my precious time watching hockey, for godsakes. But then the rats were banished, and the team started to flounder, and they fired the coach, of course, and now I've totally forgotten what icing is.

Then there's the Heat.

Say what you will about south Florida sports, we have always had the best-coiffed coaches anywhere. A fact that I don't take as a particularly good sign. For as my grandfather, a proud bald man, liked to say, "Grass doesn't grow on a busy street."

POET SINKS TO CRIME

A couple of weeks after my first novel was accepted, my new publisher sent me a twenty-five-page questionnaire. Every question was really a version of the same question: Is there anything, no matter how small or seemingly insignificant, anything at all that makes you the least bit interesting?

I dutifully filled out the questionnaire and the later questionnaires sent by my next publisher and the one after that. Much to my chagrin, all my publishers found one and only one thing interesting about me. I used to be a poet, and now I'm a crime novelist.

So for the last fifteen years, whenever I go out on a book tour and am interviewed by the handsome young man with a perfect helmet of hair, and he looks down at his notes (sent by my publisher's publicity department), the inevitable question that springs from his lips is "So, Jim, you used to be a poet and now you write crime novels. Tell us about that."

After fifteen years the question begins to have an

echoing subtext. "So, Jim, you used to be on the Supreme Court and now you're a personal injury attorney. How could you have let that happen to yourself?" "You used to be on the high road, now you're slogging along in the gutter. What happened, kid?"

I have a half-dozen answers I give to this question. The glib one is: MasterCard made me do it. The semilong one is: After writing poetry and giving poetry readings for two decades, I'd met the entire American audience for poetry. All eight hundred and forty-seven of them. I thought it was time to push on to more populated territory.

The longer and truer answer is a bit more complicated.

For twenty years I was a poet. I wrote every day, read poetry every day, published four books of poems with university presses. I didn't care that no one much reads poetry or pays money for it. Though at times I did wish MasterCard would accept for payment what I frequently received for my poetry: a free copy of the magazine my poem appeared in. My poems were published in *Poetry, Antioch Review, American Scholar, North American Review, Beloit Poetry Journal*. Magazines like that. Most people have only the vaguest knowledge of their existence. I won grants and awards, got tenure and promotion, gave readings at other universities, taught poetry to undergraduates, and in general did all the things that a successful poet does in America today.

But since I published my first novel, *Under Cover of Daylight,* in 1987, I haven't written many poems. And the fact is, I don't miss the enterprise itself. The act of composition is very similar in fiction and poetry writing. Revising and laboring over sentences, trying to find the most graceful, most economical way of saying something, searching for the right cadences of speech and the richest patterns of imagery, the simple, accessible, but meaningful observation, letting the writing lead you to discovery, flushing out the truth, then nailing it to the wall.

I sometimes tell those who ask the dreaded question that, in fact, I still do write poetry. It's just that these days the poetry goes from margin to margin rather than down the middle of the page. But in the back rooms of my secret heart, what I really want to say is: What I'm doing now—these novels I'm writing—demands more from me, challenges me artistically in ways that poetry never did.

But even more than that, I want to answer the implied snobbery in the question with a hammer blow to the forehead. After all, when is the last time my inquisitor paid for a book of poetry? When is the last time ANYBODY bought a book of poetry? While there is lip service paid to poetry, very few readers care about it. I suspect the reason for the lack of a large readership is in part that most contemporary poetry, like much mainstream fiction these days, has gone off into regions that are increasingly rarefied, increasingly divorced from the popular interests of the culture.

But writers of suspense novels have never forgotten their Dickensian responsibilities. From Hammett and MacDonald to Grafton and Leonard, it is our suspense writers who have kept alive complex plotting and rousing good yarns. Mystery novelists are practically alone in preserving rich regional settings, authentic patterns of speech, and three-dimensional minor characters. It is our crime fiction that looks square in the malevolent face of the violence and corruption that are so rife in our society. Our novelists of suspense are indeed the only group of writers today who consistently fulfill Tom Wolfe's view of the novelist's true responsibility: to write works with a wide social scope that are populated by people of all classes and to tackle the great moral and political issues of the day.

From my earliest years as a reader I was drawn to the Hardy Boys, to Nancy Drew. I never got over the sinful pleasure of reading stories about crime, adventure, the chase, the hunt, the unraveling of a deviant mind. Though my academic education was almost successful at snuffing out this enthusiasm, I managed on the sly to stay abreast of Travis and Archer and Kinsey.

Through all those years as a poet and professor, it was Elmore I took along on holidays, not Eliot. It was Thomas Harris, Sara Paretsky, Robert Parker who were my bedside reading after a day of annotating poems for tomorrow's lecture. It was Travis and Spade I returned to on weekends, not J. Alfred or Berryman's Henry.

I read Frost's poems with meticulous care in the daytime but at night frolicked through all of Ross MacDonald; explicated Wallace Stevens by day, savored James Lee Burke by moonlight, feeling superior about one, joyously guilty about the other.

If my interrogators think I have sunk low, I'd like to

see them write four hundred pages in which what happens on the last page must be prefigured in the first. Four hundred pages in which one must at every moment entertain, educate, thrill, seduce, and convince the reader it's all true. Let my interviewers take a whirl at finding untrammeled terrain in a field where there are thousands of highly competent practitioners today and a long history of accomplished writers. And let them take on a genre with millions of readers who seem to remember every damn thing ever written and who will catch you in even the most trivial errors of fact.

I used to like poetry, and I still like it. You just don't get over some diseases. But these days I don't mind admitting I write crime novels. In fact, I'm downright proud to be part of a tradition I love and respect. There! I am once and for all out of the closet.

So my absolutely final answer to the question is this: I'm a poet who also writes crime novels. One foot on the high road, one in the gutter. It makes for a lovely stride.